CHESTER
OFFICIAL GUIDE

Contents

EDITORIAL NOTE
Every effort has been made to ensure accuracy at the time of going to press. However, as changes in opening times, etc., may occur, it is advisable to check this type of information.

PHOTOGRAPHS
John Hooper, Southern Photo News and Jarrold Colour Publications, Norwich

© Chester City Council 1985

ISBN 0–7117–0155–5
Published and printed in Great Britain by Jarrold and Sons Ltd, Norwich. 185

AN INTRODUCTION TO CHESTER'S HISTORY

Origins

The 'ancient and loyal' City of Chester is 'ancient' because it was founded by the Romans; and 'loyal' because its associations with the Monarchy span 1000 years. The Romans came to Chester in the first century A.D., and founded Deva, one of the three Legionary fortresses of Roman Britain. The fortress was sited on a sandstone ridge, in a loop of the River Dee. It commanded one of the lowest crossing points of the River Dee, and was a base for the Roman fleet.

The Romans built here a typical fortress, rectangular in shape, with the **Praetorium** (or commandant's quarters) and **Principia** (headquarters building) in the centre. The Town Hall covers part of the site of the **Praetorium**. At first, buildings within the fortress were made of timber, but the Romans began to build in stone in the A.D. 70s.

Chester was first occupied by the 2nd Adiutrix Legion, but the legion principally associated with Deva was the 20th Valeria Victrix Legion, which served here for 200 years.

The fortress was smaller than the present-day walled area of the City. The inner ring road is built on the line of the fortress' western wall; and Pepper Street on its southern wall. St Michael's Church is built on part of the site of the southern gateway.

The fortress attracted a large civilian following, and a civilian settlement grew up on all sides of the fortress, except the north, where some of its cemeteries were located.

The countryside surrounding Deva was under military jurisdiction, which probably extended nearly to Whitchurch in the south. The Romans established a works depot at Holt; there was a settlement at Heronbridge, two miles south of Chester; and farms and villas were probably built alongside Roman roads.

The fortress was originally built to control the Ordovices of North Wales, and the Brigantes of northern Britain. The attitude of the local population is not known, although the Romans destroyed the early Iron Age hillfort at Eddisbury. However, over the centuries, considerable intermarriage is likely to have taken place.

Anglo-Saxon Chester

In the late ninth century, the *Anglo-Saxon Chronicle* describes Chester as 'a deserted Roman site in Wirral called Legaceaster'. However, archaeologists are

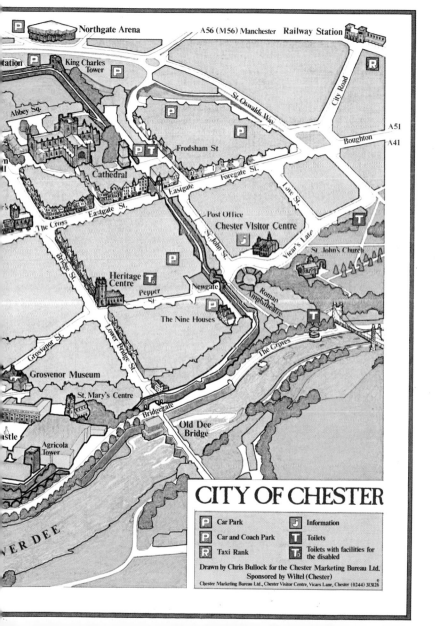

CITY OF CHESTER

P	Car Park	J	Information
P	Car and Coach Park	T	Toilets
R	Taxi Rank	T♿	Toilets with facilities for the disabled

Drawn by Chris Bullock for the Chester Marketing Bureau Ltd.
Sponsored by Wiltel (Chester)
Chester Marketing Bureau Ltd., Chester Visitor Centre, Vicars Lane, Chester (0244) 313126

beginning to believe that Chester was never completely abandoned; and at the beginning of the tenth century, it was refortified by Aethelflaeda, Lady of the Mercians.

Aethelflaeda was a daughter of King Alfred the Great of Wessex. She married Aethelred, Ealdorman of Mercia, but even before his death in 911, she took a prominent part in the campaigns against the Vikings. In Chester in 907, Aethelflaeda possibly extended the walls of the Roman fortress to the line of the present City walls; and she built a chain of fortresses stretching from Eddisbury and Runcorn, to the Pennines.

There is some reason to believe that Lower Bridge Street was the focal point of Aethelflaeda's **burh** (fortified town).

Anglo-Saxon Chester became a rich and prosperous community. Tradition says that the bones of St Werburgh were brought to Chester from Hanbury in Staffordshire, in 875, to protect them from Danish attack. As well as St Werburgh's Church, churches dedicated to St Peter (at the centre of Chester), and St John (east of the Roman amphitheatre site), had been founded by the middle tenth century. There were also moneyers in Chester producing silver coins; and in 973 King Edgar came to Chester after his Coronation at Bath, and was rowed on the River Dee by Celtic kings, who recognised him as their overlord.

The Domesday Book describes this community in the time of King Edward the Confessor when there were 487 houses in Chester. There was a sophisticated system of justice, controlled by judges:

> There were then 12 judges of the city . . . If any of them absented himself from the Hundred (court) on the day of its session without sufficient excuse, he paid a fine of 10 shillings to the king and the earl.

In addition, Chester was also a thriving port:

> If ships arrived at or departed from the port of the city without the king's licence, the king and the earl had 40 shillings from each man who was on the ships.

> If a ship came against the king's peace and in spite of his prohibition, the king and the earl had both the ship and the men and all that was in it.

Medieval Chester

After the death of King Edward the Confessor, the English throne was claimed by William of Normandy, who defeated Harold at the Battle of Hastings in 1066. William's conquest of England was gradual, and bitterly resisted. He laid waste Cheshire in the winter of 1069–70; and gave responsibility for controlling it to Hugh of Avranches, nicknamed Lupus, who became Earl of Chester *circa* 1077. Hugh divided Cheshire among eight barons, who in their turn, subdivided it among their followers. They ruled the local population from their castles.

Chester Castle, begun by William the Conqueror, became the centre of the Earldom of Chester. The Norman earls were among the most powerful in the kingdom. Earl Ranulph III for a time claimed the title Duke of Brittany. However, when the 7th Norman Earl, John the Scot, died in 1237, the Earldom reverted to the Crown. In 1254, Henry III granted Cheshire to his elder son, the Lord Edward, who lost it for two years during the Barons' War to Simon de Montfort, until Simon's defeat and death at the Battle of Evesham in 1265. Since 1301, the heir to the throne has usually held the titles Prince of Wales and Earl of Chester.

Until Edward I's conquest of North Wales, Chester Castle was the starting point for many expeditions against the Welsh. There was one led by King John in 1211; a highly unsuccessful campaign by Henry III in 1245; and in 1277 Edward I began his campaign against Prince Llywelyn ap Gruffydd, by crossing the Dee via the ford at Shotwick, five miles north-west of Chester.

With the conquest of North Wales, the Welsh danger to Chester diminished, although unrest continued throughout the Middle Ages. In 1402, during Owain Glyndŵr's uprising, the Mayor and Sheriffs were ordered to assist the Royal cause in North Wales, by going to sea in a barge called the *Trinity of Chester*, and three other fully armed vessels; and as late as 1516, Chester people were forbidden by the City Assembly, to attend Welsh weddings.

Medieval Chester was a busy, cosmopolitan port. The monk Lucian, writing *circa* 1195, declared:

> *Our Chester has also, by the favour of God, a rich and graceful river beneath the City walls, beautiful and abounding in fish, and on its South side a harbour for ships coming from Aquitaine, Spain, Ireland, and Germany, which by Christ's guidance and by the labour and skill of the merchants, come and unload at the City bay with many goods, so that, comforted in all ways by the grace of our God, we may drink wine more often and more plentifully . . .*

Lucian was a monk of St Werburgh's, which had been refounded as a Benedictine Abbey by Earl Hugh I in 1092. The Abbey and its precincts occupied almost a quarter of the area within the City walls. It owned thirteen houses in Chester in 1086, and had property throughout Cheshire. There was also a Priory of Benedictine Nuns, established near the Castle in the middle twelfth century.

The Franciscan, Dominican, and Carmelite Friars also established houses in Chester. Both the Franciscan and Dominican houses were situated near to the Watergate, and the port. There were two hospitals outside the City walls. St John-without-the-Northgate was probably founded by Earl Ranulph III in the 1190s. He may also have founded the leper hospital at Spital Boughton, which was dedicated to St Giles.

Medieval Chester was also served by nine parish churches. In addition to St Werburgh's Church, the monk Lucian, *circa* 1195, mentions St Peter's, St John's, and St Michael's. Until Henry VIII's reformation of the English church, St John's was a collegiate church, served by a dean, seven canons, and four

Godstall Lane

Right: Chester Town Crier, the Cross

minor canons. St Michael's, at the corner of Bridge Street and Pepper Street, is first mentioned in a charter granted to Norton Priory *circa* 1154–60. One of the most interesting churches in Chester is St Olave's in Lower Bridge Street, dedicated to St Olaf, King of Norway (died 1030), betraying Scandinavian influence in Chester.

City State

The government of Chester came to be controlled by its citizens. William Smith, writing *circa* 1575, claimed that:

> *The Estate that the Maior of Chester kepeth is great. ffor he hath both Swordbearer, Macebearer Serjeants with their Silver Maces, in as good and Decent order, as in any other Cittie of England . . .*

The first Mayor of Chester is said to have been William the Clerk in 1238. The office of Sheriff is the earliest in the country, dating from the 1120s. Chester had two Sheriffs appointed annually, until the Municipal Corporations Act of 1835.

The development of the citizens' power depended on the grant of charter privileges. Charters were granted either by the King, or the Earl of Chester. The first Royal charter, granted *circa* 1175–76, confirms trading rights in Dublin. However, it was Edward I's charter of 1300, granting Chester to the citizens, in

return for a fee farm rent of £100 per annum, which encouraged the development of the machinery of government. Its fully developed form was recognised by Henry VII's 'Great Charter' of 1506. This provided for an Assembly of Mayor, two Sheriffs, twenty-four Aldermen, and forty Common Councilmen. In addition, Chester was granted its own Court of Quarter Sessions; the Mayor was granted the right to 'have their sword which we gave them . . . carried before them with the point upright'; and for most purposes, the charter recognised Chester's independence of the rest of Cheshire. In Tudor times, the City's privileges were guarded jealously; the Mayor and Sheriffs upheld their dignity; and Chester became almost the equivalent of an Italian city state.

Alongside City government, the City guilds or companies began to emerge in the Middle Ages. In 1475, there were nineteen companies. Twenty-three companies survive to the present day. The companies were formed to protect different crafts. They regulated wages and prices, and looked after their poor. Before 1506, they received charters only from the King or the Earl of Chester. For example, in 1362, the Tanners received a charter which forbade the Cordwainers from meddling with their trade. After 1506, the Assembly attempted to control the companies, and charters were granted by the Mayor and Citizens. In 1534, such a charter united the Painters, Glaziers, Embroiderers and Stationers, into one company.

Between City government and companies, there must have been interdependence; and for individuals, conflicts of interest. Usually, an Alderman or Steward of a company, was also either an Alderman or Common Councilman of the City.

The companies contributed to the pageantry of Medieval and Tudor Chester. They produced the Chester Cycle of Mystery Plays, which perhaps date from the last quarter of the fourteenth century. The tradition that they were written by Ranulph Higden, monk of St Werburgh's Abbey, who died in 1364, has been disproved. The plays were performed over three days, in the sixteenth century at Whitsun. They were announced by a ceremony known as 'the Ryddyng of the banes'; and the Mayor issued a proclamation commanding everyone who resorted to the plays, to keep the peace. The plays were performed at different stations throughout Chester. They began outside the Abbey Gateway, and moved next to the High Cross in front of St Peter's, for a performance in front of the Mayor and other civic dignitaries. The plays were performed on carriages described as:

a howse with 2 rowmes being open on the tope the lower rowme theie apparrelled and dressed themselves and the higher rowme they played and thei stoode upon vi wheeles . . .

Until 1951, the plays were performed for the last time in Chester in 1575. They had been banned by the Archbishop of York, because of their associations with the Roman Catholic Church; and growing Puritan feeling in Chester was also opposed to them.

Civil War

The quarrel between Charles I and his Parliament, which became war in 1642, had a profound effect on Chester. There was a Puritan faction in the City Assembly, but the Gamull family, who were Royalists, retained control. Sir William Brereton was ejected from the city when he attempted to raise troops for Parliament in 1642; and Chester declared for the King.

Charles I came to Chester on two occasions: in 1642; and in 1645, when his army was defeated on Rowton Moor. The King retreated into Wales; the siege of Chester continued, and Chester surrendered to the Parliamentary forces in February 1646.

Randle Holme, author of *The Academy of Armory*, lists the destruction caused by the siege. This included:

> In the Foregate Street, Cow-lane, St. John's Lane, with those houses next to the Eastgate, all burned to the ground . . . The destruction of divers other houses in the cittie, with grenadoes, not a house from Eastgate to the middle of Watergate street on both sides but received some hurt by them, many sleyne by the fall of houses which were blown up, St. Peter's Church much defaced and pews torne, and all windows broken by two grenadoes that fell therein . . .

Not surprisingly, the siege placed intolerable burdens on the City Treasury; and Chester was also expected to subscribe to the Royal cause. The City possessed a fine collection of silver. On 31 January 1645, the Assembly ordered that £100 worth of plate be melted down and converted 'into Coyne for the necessarie use and defence of this Citty . . .'

Decline and Resurgence

Chester's prosperity had begun to decline before the Civil War. As early as 1484, the citizens complained to the King:

> . . . the great flow of water at the said port . . . is taken away owing to the wreck of sea sands daily falling and increasing in the channel there, so that the said port is wholly destroyed and cannot be recovered, insomuch that no merchant ship can approach the said city for twelve miles and more.

Although this complaint was probably exaggerated, the channel of the River Dee was gradually silting up. In the sixteenth century, a New Haven was built at Parkgate, ten miles downstream from Chester; and a new channel was cut in the river in 1735–36. The New Cut was intended to make the Dee navigable for ships of 200 tons, from the sea to Chester. Unfortunately, this scheme was only a partial success.

The building of the Chester Canal in the 1770s was another attempt to revive Chester's trade. The proprietors aimed to build a canal from Chester to join the Trent and Mersey Canal at Middlewich. The canal was completed as far as Nantwich by 1779, but the Middlewich branch was not built until the

Old Dee Bridge and Weir

1830s. One canal historian has described the Chester Canal as 'the first thoroughly unsuccessful canal'.

Nevertheless, the canal helped the establishment of industries in Chester in the late eighteenth and early nineteenth centuries, notably the leadworks of Messrs Walker, Parker and Company, producing lead shot; and the Flookersbrook Foundry, which became the Hydraulic Engineering Company in 1874. Both contributed to Britain's success in the Napoleonic Wars. By the end of the wars in 1815, there were three shipyards on the Roodee, employing 250 people. During the war, 'several vessels of war were built here, carrying about 24 guns each'.

Modern Chester

Commerce and industry changed the physical appearance of Chester. The New Cut changed the course of the River Dee, creating the sharp angled bend about one mile north of the City walls. A second bridge was built across the River Dee. The Dee Bridge linking Chester and Handbridge, which may be Roman in origin, was described by Thomas Pennant in 1773 as 'very narrow and dangerous'. A private Act of Parliament was obtained in 1825, which authorised the building of the Grosvenor Bridge, opened by Princess Victoria in 1832. At that time, the largest single arch stone bridge in the world, it improved communications between Chester and North Wales.

The building of the Grosvenor Bridge caused the first change in Chester's Romano-Medieval street pattern. St Bridget's Church, at the corner of Bridge Street and White Friars, was demolished; and a new street, named Grosvenor Street, was built to link Bridge Street with the new bridge.

The railways also made many changes to Chester's physical appearance. The railway lines from Chester to Birkenhead, and from Chester to Crewe, were opened in 1840. An early plan to site their terminal next to Chester Cathedral, was abandoned. The General Railway Station, on the north-eastern side of the City, was built in 1847–48; and City Road was built in the early 1860s, to link the station and Foregate Street. It was decorated with a triumphal arch when the Prince of Wales came to Chester to open the new Town Hall in 1869.

The Railway Station was near the industrial areas of the City, and streets of small, terraced houses surrounded it: in Hoole to the east; and in Newtown to the north-west. Chester's poverty was, however, most apparent in the courts alongside Foregate Street, and at the back of the Town Hall. Here, people lived in small, dilapidated cottages which were crowded together. There were frequent outbreaks of typhus fever and other diseases. Improvements were made gradually: water closets replaced 'the offensive midden closet' in 1878; and most of the courts had been demolished by the 1930s, the population moving out to the new suburbs of Lache, Newton, and Blacon.

Elsewhere, there was evidence of Chester's wealth and status. Joseph Hemingway, Editor of the *Chester Chronicle* from 1824 to 1830, compared Eastgate Street with Regent Street in London; and Browns of Chester was later described as the 'Harrods of the North'. Bolland and Sons were confectioners to H.M. Queen Victoria, and H.R.H. The Prince of Wales.

Many of Chester's buildings were rebuilt in the second half of the nineteenth century. Sir Nikolaus Pevsner and Edward Hubbard, writing in 1971, assert:

> Chester is not a medieval, it is a Victorian city. What deceives is the black and white. 95 per cent is Victorian and after. It is able to deceive because the motifs are accurately imitated . . .

Chester's 'black and white' appearance was created by such architects as John Douglas and Thomas Meakin Lockwood. Douglas designed St Werburgh's Mount, opposite the Cathedral; and rebuilt the east side of St Werburgh Street in the 1890s; and Lockwood created the distinctive buildings on both corners of Bridge Street, at The Cross.

The appearance of Chester Cathedral, whose 'distintegration was proverbially spoken of throughout England', was also changed in the nineteenth century. The principal works were designed by Sir George Gilbert Scott, who added flying buttresses and battlemented parapets, between 1868 and 1876.

Chester has attracted tourists from an early date. The first guide book to Chester was published in 1781. In the nineteenth century, Liverpool was the main port of entry for American visitors, and an American scholar has written:

> In the morning, pausing only to be horrified by the poverty and squalor that Liverpool presented, and for which Dickens seems never adequately to have prepared him, he (the American traveller) fled thankfully to Chester for his first taste of antiquity and romance.

A late nineteenth-century guide book declared 'that Chester can hold its own among the cities of the kingdom' for hotel accommodation; and visitors with only a short time to spend in Chester were advised to take a tram ride from the General Station to the Grosvenor Bridge, to see 'a hasty glimpse of the Rows and quaint houses and streets . . .'

In 1979, Chester celebrated 1900 Years of History, 'a remarkable achievement and well worthy of celebration'. H.R.H. The Prince of Wales visited Chester in July 1979; and H.M. The Queen and H.R.H. Prince Philip attended a special Service of Thanksgiving in Chester Cathedral on 2 November. Cestrians and visitors watched the Royal procession from the Town Hall to the Cathedral.

H.M. Queen Elizabeth II has granted two charters to Chester. On 1 April 1974, the City of Chester, independent of the County for nearly 500 years, was amalgamated with the adjoining Rural Districts of Chester and Tarvin; this area became one of eight new Cheshire Districts created by Local Government Reorganisation. The two charters, granted in 1974, allow Chester to retain many of its ancient privileges. Its first citizen is still entitled Mayor; he is also Admiral of the Dee; he may still have his sword carried before him with the point upright; and an area of 173 square miles, enjoys the title 'City of Chester'.

Bridge Street

Left: Tudor House, Lower Bridge Street

A TOUR OF
HISTORIC CHESTER

The antiquary, Thomas Hughes, wrote about Chester in the nineteenth century:

> The eye of the stranger, be he Englishman or foreigner, European or American, will here find an ample and luxuriant field for admiration: the man of taste, who may linger within its walls, will not depart ungratified; nor will the antiquary search here in vain for some rich and profitable treasures of investigation.

These 'treasures of investigation' are all within walking distance of Chester's Victorian Town Hall, which houses the Tourist Information Centre, at street level, fronting the Market Square. Walking tours of the City, led by Chester's voluntary guides, start from the Town Hall. The tour which follows is not necessarily the route which the guides would take. Rather, it aims to descibe, in a logical order, Chester's historic sites.

CHESTER TOWN HALL, in the Market Square, was built in 1865–69. It was opened by H.R.H. The Prince of Wales on 15 October 1869. It replaced a late seventeenth-century Town Hall, known as the Exchange, which was destroyed by fire in 1862. The best known feature of the Exchange was a statue of Queen Anne, by the sculptor, John Tilston, which stood in a central niche.

The 'new' Town Hall was designed by the architect, William Henry Lynn of Belfast, who won a public competition. Designs by Alfred Waterhouse, architect of Manchester Town Hall, and Eaton Hall, seat of the Duke of Westminster, which was demolished in the 1960s, were rejected.

The Town Hall is built in the Gothic style. Its exterior consists of bands of red and grey sandstone; and a central tower rises to a height of 160 feet. The clock, on three faces of the tower, commemorates Chester's 1900th Anniversary, celebrated in 1979.

The **Main Entrance** of the Town Hall is approached by two flights of steps from the Market Square. The date 1869, and Chester's former Armorial Bearings, are carved above the double entrance doors. In the **Porch**, there are also four panel sculptures in Bath stone, depicting scenes from Chester's history.

The **Waiting Hall** and its central staircase, which divides it into two, are among the finest features of the Town Hall. There are fine wooden ceilings; panel sculptures above the main doorways; and a circular stained-glass window, depicting the common seal of the City, set high above the eastern end of the inner hall. Also in the inner hall, a war memorial bears the names of over 700 Cestrians killed in the Great War, 1914–19. This was erected by Sir John Meadows Frost, Mayor, 1914–19, 'in memory of a beloved son', Captain T. L. Frost, who was killed in action in 1915. Two Cheshire Regiment flags hang above the entrance doors into the Assembly Room.

The Chester Tapestry decorates the walls of the inner hall. Inspired by European Architectural Heritage Year, 1975, the theme of the tapestry is 'Chester Today'. It depicts Chester's walls and gates, the Roodee, Chester Zoo, and the rural areas around the City. The River Dee meanders through the whole. The tapestry was designed by Diana Springall. It was embroidered by about 200 workers, and Wilton carpet wool of white, pink, red, brown, and black, the colours typical of Chester, was used.

The **Assembly Room** is the largest room in the Town Hall. Its walls are partially panelled. Chester's former Armorial Bearings, and the City's motto 'Antiqui Colant Antiquum Dierum' ('Let the Ancients Worship the Ancient of Days'), are painted high above the stage. There is another fine stained-glass window, and portraits of nine members of the Grosvenor family are hung here. These include Sir Thomas Grosvenor, 3rd Baronet, who was Mayor in 1684–85, and Member of Parliament for Chester in 1679–80 and 1685–88. He married the heiress Mary Davies, and acquired her manor of Ebury, which included Mayfair and Belgravia in London. His portrait is attributed to Sir Godfrey Kneller. There are two portraits by the American artist Benjamin West, of Richard, 1st Earl Grosvenor, Mayor in 1759–60, and of Thomas Grosvenor, Esquire, Mayor in 1760–61. There are also portraits of Richard, 2nd Marquess of Westminster, and Hugh Lupus, 1st Duke of Westminster, generous benefactors of the City.

A painting by Arthur Burgess of the light cruiser, H.M.S. *Chester*, also hangs in the Assembly Room. She was built by Cammell Laird and Company at Birkenhead; and the painting shows her leaving the Mersey on her first voyage. H.M.S. *Chester* fought in the Battle of Jutland in 1916. One of her crew was John Travers Cornwell, aged 16, who was posthumously awarded the Victoria Cross for his heroism during the battle.

The **Court Room**, which also leads off the waiting hall, is used as a Magistrates' Court. Until 1971, meetings of Chester City Court of Quarter Sessions were held here, and a plaque records the last sitting of the court on 23 November 1971. A full-size portrait of King George III, by John Jackson, hangs above the magistrates' bench.

The **Staircase** in the waiting hall leads to a half landing and balcony. On the half landing, there is a memorial carved in Portland stone, which was presented to the City of Chester by the Polish Air Force Unit at Sealand, on Poland's National Day, 3 August 1944.

At the top of the staircase, there are portraits of the seven Norman earls of Chester; and also a portrait of Edric Sylvestris described as 'Ancestor to the Sylvesters of Stourton in Wirral'. They are shown wearing Tudor armour, and were painted in 1578. The portraits were purchased by Sir Thomas Gibbons Frost in 1883; and he presented them to the City.

*Far right:
The Rows,
Watergate Street*

*Right: Three
Old Arches,
Bridge Street*

Three Old Arches

1274 AD   1274 AD

owen owen

*Below: Town
Hall Square*

Above the staircase, there are eight Victorian stained-glass windows, each containing a portrait of an Earl of Chester.

The second floor of the Town Hall contains the Council Chamber, Mayoral suite, and Committee Room. The **Council Chamber** is oak panelled, with a fine wooden ceiling, and carvings in wood and stone. It was destroyed by fire in 1897, but restored by the architect, T. M. Lockwood, in the following year.

Chester City Council meets every six weeks in the Council Chamber. There are sixty elected members, and the Mayor acts as Chairman. He sits on a dais, in a large, carved chair which dates from 1869, with the Deputy Mayor on his left, and the Chief Executive and Director of Finance on his right. The chief Executive retains the title of Town Clerk, for ceremonial purposes. The Sheriff, who seals the official documents of the City, sits in a similar chair, at the opposite end of the Chamber, to the Mayor. Provision is made for members of the press and public to attend Council meetings.

There are brackets on the wall of the Council Chamber where the City Sword and Mace are placed when the Council is in session. While the Sword probably dates from the fifteenth century, its scabbard, and the Mace, were presented to Chester by Charles, Earl of Derby, who was Mayor in 1668–69. Chester's Sword was used to perform the investiture of the Prince of Wales at Caernarfon Castle in 1911. The Mace is made of silver gilt. Its head, surmounted by a crown, is decorated with a Tudor rose, a harp, a thistle, and a fleur de lis, which symbolise England, Ireland, Scotland, and France. Its shaft is divided by massive knobs, and decorated with roses and thistles.

The silver Admiralty Oar is used when the Mayor acts as Admiral of the Dee. It has a blade fourteen inches long, and was made by the Chester goldsmith, Richard Richardson I, in 1719–20.

The insignia of office include the Mayor's gold Chain, for day wear, with its massive gold links, and badge which incorporates the City Coat of Arms. It was presented by John Williams in 1851. The Sheriff's Chain is similar, lacking only the crossed sword and mace of the Mayor's Chain. It was presented to Chester by Alderman Francis Butt in 1869, on the occasion of the opening of the Town Hall. The Mayor's Evening Badge, a large gold medallion surrounded by diamonds, was presented in 1890 by Miss Nessie Brown, when her brother, Charles Brown, became Mayor of Chester for the fourth time.

Letters Patent granting Chester's Armorial Bearings, are also on display in the Council Chamber. These were granted to the City on 10 March 1977 (for a description **see** page 53).

The **Mayor's Parlour** was redecorated in 1977. A few items from the City's fine collection of silver, are on display here. The **Mayoress' Parlour**, adjoining it, contains nine portraits on panelling, of founders of the City Charities. The portraits date from the seventeenth and eighteenth centuries. They were originally in the Exchange, but were rescued from the fire of 1862. The Mayoress' Parlour also contains one of the H.M.S. *Chester* clocks. Six clocks, carved in oak, and resembling the west front of Chester Cathedral, were presented to H.M.S. *Chester* by the citizens in May 1916. A large clock, of similar design, was presented to the ship by Chester's Member of Parliament, Robert Yerburgh. When H.M.S. *Chester* was scrapped in 1921, the clocks returned to the City.

The **Committee Room**, which adjoins the Mayor's Parlour on the other side, is noted for its panelling bearing the names of the Mayors of Chester from 1238.

When the Council meets, or when the Mayor receives important visitors, the Civil Flag is flown. This is ten feet by eight feet in size, and represents the Armorial Bearings granted to Chester in 1977. The flag was designed by Mr T. Alan Keith-Hill, an heraldic expert, and made by Porter Brothers of Liverpool, in 1980.

Visitors to the Town Hall must remember that it is not a museum: it houses City Council Departments; the offices of the Clerk to the Chester City Justices; and all its public rooms are in frequent use. Since the Mayor's permission must be obtained for visits to the Mayoral suite, tours of the Town Hall are best arranged by contacting the Mayor's Secretary.

The **Ground Floor**, or basement, of the Town Hall was originally the City Police Station. Although they still use a part of the basement in connection with the Magistrates' Courts, the Police moved to new headquarters opposite Chester Castle in 1967. Another part of the basement is occupied by the **Chester City Record Office**, which is responsible for Chester's records and archives. These are among the City's greatest treasures. They range in date from *circa* 1175 to the present day; occupy approximately one mile of shelving; and contain a wealth of information about Chester's history. The Record Office is open to the public. It provides a Search Room, where members of the public may consult the records; there is also a small reference library; and help and guidance from experts is always available. There is also an educational programme for schools.

The **Tourist Information Centre** adjoins the Record Office, in the south-eastern corner of the Town Hall. It incorporates a wall built out of Roman masonry, recovered from excavations on the former taxi rank in Princess Street, in 1980. This masonry was part of a large central building in the Roman fortress, possibly the Praetorium. It has been reconstructed to match an existing wall, dating from 1869.

When visitors leave the Town Hall to begin their imaginary tour, they will find themselves on the **MARKET SQUARE**, which is surrounded by a variety of architectural styles. If they look to the south, they will see **The Forum**. This is a sharp contrast to the Town Hall. It is a modern complex of shops and Council offices, and leads to the Gateway Theatre, and to the covered market at the rear of the Town Hall. This was an area redeveloped in the late 1960s and early 1970s. The Forum replaced a Victorian Market with a baroque façade. This was designed by the architect, James M. Hay of Liverpool, who won a public competition. The Market was opened in 1863. Traces of its façade may be seen adjoining the **Dublin Packet**, and the alley leading to **Hamilton Place**. Remains of the Roman strongroom in the **Principia**, are displayed in the wall of The Forum in Hamilton Place.

Roman Soldier, Wall Patrol

Looking north from the Town Hall, the visitor will see the building once occupied by the '**Westminster Coach and Motor Car Works**'. In the nineteenth and early part of the twentieth century, this was the home of the coach building firms of William Hewitt and J. A. Lawton. It was partially destroyed by fire in 1903, and rebuilt. Although its site is scheduled for redevelopment, its façade will be retained.

The **Odeon Cinema**, on the corner of the Market Square and Hunter Street, was opened in 1936 on the site of Northgate House, an eighteenth-century house which was the home and office of the Potts family, solicitors and Clerks to Cheshire County Council from 1889 to 1931. The houses and shops on the eastern side of the Market Square are mostly eighteenth century, although there are modern infills.

The buildings on the eastern side of the Market Square, directly opposite the Town Hall, are the most impressive. **Barclays Bank** was designed by the architect, Sir Arthur W. Blomfield, for the King's School, which moved there in 1876. The King's School, the oldest school in Chester, was formerly housed in the Cathedral Refectory. It was founded by Henry VIII in 1541, after the dissolution of the Abbey of St Werburgh, to educate 24 'poor and friendless boys', but it later became a school for the sons of prosperous townspeople, and local gentry. By 1960, the school was too large for its premises, and it moved to new buildings on the Wrexham Road. The old King's School adjoins the **Abbey Gateway**, which dates from the fourteenth century, although there are later additions.

Abbey Gateway leads into **ABBEY SQUARE**. This is a pleasant area within the Cathedral precincts, with stone paved carriage ways and cobbles surrounding grass. In the centre of the grass, is a pillar which is said to have come from the Exchange (**see** page 18). The houses on the west side of Abbey Square are eighteenth to early nineteenth century in date. On the north, they are eighteenth century, although their façades, particularly in the case of the Retreat House (Nos. 10–11), conceal earlier features. On the east side of Abbey Square, there is a detached house of the mid eighteenth century, which has a rainwater head bearing the date 1754. Adjoining it are two cottages built of sandstone, which date from 1626. These are built on the site of the Abbey kitchens.

From Abbey Square, the visitor should walk eastwards along **ABBEY STREET** to the City walls. The Bishop's House, with its walled garden in front, is on the corner of Abbey Square and Abbey Street. It dates from the late eighteenth century. Other houses on the north side of Abbey Street are particularly fine examples of eighteenth-century architecture, recently restored. Nos. 5–7 have a rainwater head dated 1764, and both carry fire insurance plaques.

From Abbey Street, the visitor can either pass through the doorway known as **Kaleyards Gate**, or climb on to the City walls. Tradition says that Edward I allowed the monks of St Werburgh's Abbey to make this breach in the City walls about 1275. Control of the gate passed from the monks to the Dean and Chapter of Chester Cathedral. It is still locked at 9 o'clock each evening. Traces of the original Roman wall can be seen in the Kaleyards, to the south of the Kaleyards Gate.

The **CITY WALLS** above Kaleyards Gate are a splendid vantage point. To the north is **King Charles' Tower**, so named because Charles I watched from there in September 1645, as his army was defeated by the Parliamentarians at the Battle of Rowton Moor. King Charles' Tower has also been called Newton's and the Phoenix Tower. The phoenix is the emblem of the Painters, Glaziers, Embroiderers and Stationers Company, who used this tower as a meeting house in the seventeenth century. A phoenix, and the date 1613, are carved above the door at wall level. Stairs lead to an upper room, which houses a museum devoted to the Civil War. A cartouche depicting the Armorial Bearings of the Painters, Glaziers, Embroiderers and Stationers Company, is placed above the doorway to the upper room.

From the Kaleyards Gate, there is also a view eastward towards **Frodsham Street** and the newly developed area between Frodsham Street and **Queen Street**. Until the nineteenth century, Frodsham Street was known as Cow Lane, possibly because most of the City's slaughter houses were sited there. Cow Lane Bridge, over the canal, rebuilt in 1959–60, links Frodsham Street with the **Gorsestacks**. In the seventeenth century, the City bakers were ordered to stack their firewood there, because of the fire hazard to the thatched houses within the City walls. A cattle market was built at the Gorsestacks in 1850, after complaints from the residents of Upper Northgate Street, where the cattle market was formerly held. The cattle market at the Gorsestacks was closed in 1970, and demolished. It was replaced by a modern complex on the Sealand Trading Estate, $1\frac{1}{2}$ miles to the west of the City centre.

The area between Frodsham Street and Queen Street was known as the **Jousting Croft**. It is first mentioned in the City Records in 1472, and tradition asserts that tournaments were held there. The new Tesco Superstore is built on part of the Jousting Croft. An early eighteenth century Friends Meeting House in Frodsham Street, was demolished in the early 1970s.

Very little remains of **Queen Street** and its elegant Georgian terraced houses. The classical façade of **Queen Street Congregational Church**, built in 1776–77, has been incorporated in the Tesco Superstore. This was one of the earliest chapels in Chester. Its first members were a breakaway group from Matthew Henry's Chapel, built in Trinity Street in 1699–1700. Part of Boots the Chemists occupies the site of the Roman Catholic Church and schools on the west side of Queen Street. The church was built in 1799, and the schools in 1854. A new St Werburgh's Church was built in Grosvenor Park Road in 1875, and the schools closed in 1968. Burial grounds associated with the churches in Queen Street were closed in 1855, but remains were found when the sites was cleared for redevelopment.

Walking south from the Kaleyards Gate, the visitor should pause where the wall adjoins **MERCIA SQUARE**, named after the Anglo-Saxon Kingdom of Mercia. Another modern development, this is built partly on the site of the Hop

The Groves and River Dee

Eastgate Street

Pole Paddock, which the City intended to use for horse fairs in the late nineteenth century. From here, you may also look down on **Chester Cathedral Garden**; and admire the battlements and turrets added to the Cathedral by Sir George Gilbert Scott during the restoration of the nineteenth century.

A short distance south along the wall from Mercia Square, the visitor reaches Chester's most photographed features: the **EASTGATE** and the **Eastgate Clock**. The present Eastgate was built in 1768–69. An inscription records that it was built at the expense of Richard, Lord Grosvenor. The medieval gate which it replaced, is said to have incorporated Roman arches; and traces of the eastern gateway of the Roman fortress were found during repairs to a sewer in 1972. Tolls were originally charged on goods entering Chester through each of its gates. Those at the Eastgate were not collected by the City Authorities. The Serjeancy of the Eastgate was originally granted by Edward I to Henry de Bradford in 1274. The Serjeancy later passed to the Earl of Oxford, and finally to the Marquess of Crewe.

The Eastgate Clock was erected in 1899 to commemorate Queen Victoria's Diamond Jubilee. Its iron framework was designed by the architect, John Douglas; the clock was made by J. B. Joyce of Whitchurch; and presented by Colonel Edward Evans-Lloyd, 'Citizen and Freeman'.

The Eastgate commands a splendid view of both Eastgate Street and Foregate Street. **FOREGATE STREET** was the Roman Watling Street, and a civilian community settled alongside it. Its buildings are a mixture of styles. On the south side, No. 70 which is timber framed, overhangs the pavement, and is supported by timber columns. It is said to date from 1571. C & A Modes adjoining it, was opened in 1972. This was built on the site of the Classic Cinema and Swan Hotel. On the northern side of Foregate Street, the front of Boots the Chemists, opened in 1980, incorporates the façade of the Old Nag's Head. This was built in 1597, and rebuilt in 1914. The whole is an imaginative and successful attempt to blend old and new.

EASTGATE STREET was the eastern section of the Roman Via Principalis. On the south side, adjoining the Eastgate, is the **Grosvenor Hotel**. This was built between 1863 and 1866 on the site of the Royal Hotel. It was named Grosvenor Hotel, in honour of Richard, 2nd Marquess of Westminster, who owned it. The architect of the Grosvenor Hotel was T. M. Penson, one of the first exponents of the half timber revival.

Originally, **Newgate Street** alongside the Grosvenor Hotel, linked Eastgate Street and Pepper Street. It is now one of the pedestrian entrances to the **Grosvenor-Laing Shopping Precinct**, opened in 1965. Until the eighteenth century, Newgate Street was known as Fleshmongers Lane.

Browns of Chester is also on the south side of Eastgate Street. It was founded by Susannah Brown in the late eighteenth century, and became one of the best known shops in the north. The building has three distinctive architectural styles. In the middle, there is a classical façade, erected *circa* 1828. To the west of the classical façade, is the building erected by T. M. Penson in 1858, an early example of high Victorian Gothic, with a central tower. This building was intended to blend with the thirteenth-century crypt beneath it. To the east of the classical façade, is a half-timbered building, dating from the middle nineteenth century.

There are several interesting buildings on the north side of Eastgate Street. The **Midland Bank**, adjoining the Eastgate, is a red brick building designed by John Douglas, in a Dutch of Flemish style. It was built to house the Grosvenor Club; and the North and South Wales Bank. It bears the date 1883, and it is decorated with Armorial Bearings, including the early arms of the Grosvenor family: a gold wheatsheaf on a blue background (azure a garb or).

Barclays Bank, on the eastern corner of Eastgate Street and St Werburgh Street, is the end of a range of buildings designed as a town planning exercise by John Douglas in the 1890s. The **National Westminster Bank** on the opposite corner, was built by George Williams in 1859 60, in a classical style. Further west, the **Boot Inn**, one of the oldest in Chester, dates from the seventeenth century. Near Here, a Roman altar was found in 1861 on the site of **Duttons' Sigano Stores**

A short distance south of the Eastgate is the ruined Wolf Tower which dates from the fourteenth century. It is also known as **Thimbleby's Tower**. This is a short distance from the **NEWGATE**, a modern structure, and another excellent vantage point. The Newgate has a wide stone archway, flanked by towers. It bears the Armorial Bearings of the Prince of Wales, and the Grosvenor Family on the west, and the Arms of the Stanleys and Egertons on the east. It was designed by Sir Walter Tapper, and opened in 1930.

The Newgate is built alongside the **Wolf Gate** or **Pepper Gate**, which had become a hazard to modern traffic. This was rebuilt in 1608. Legend associates it with the elopement of Alderman Ralph Aldersey's daughter, Ellen. In 1573, the City Assembly ordered the stopping up of the Wolf Gate by day and night. It was reopened in the following year.

This area is rich in Roman remains. The Wolf Gate stands on part of the south-east corner of the Roman fortress. A **garden** was laid out, just outside the Newgate, in 1949, and part of a Roman hypocaust, or heating system, was re-constructed there. In addition, the northern half of the **Roman amphitheatre**, was excavated in 1929–34 and 1965–69. This played an important part in the social life of Roman Chester. The oval arena is thought to have measured 190 by 162 feet; and there was accommodation for 7000 people. There was a bear pit on this site in the eighteenth century; and the Volunteer Rifle Brigade practised here in the 1860s.

Opposite the amphitheatre is **CHESTER VISITOR CENTRE**. This was originally opened in 1974 and totally revamped and reopened in May 1984 in the former Grosvenor St John's Schools. The schools dated from 1813. The building now occupied by the Chester Visitor Centre was built in the 1880s by the school architect, E. R. Robson, and now houses a Tourist Information Centre, bureau de change, video show and a life-size reconstruction of the Rows of Chester in Victorian days, together with a licensed restaurant and craft shop.

31

Eastgate Clock

Chester Visitor Centre

To the east of the amphitheatre is **ST JOHN'S CHURCH** and **Ruins**. St John's Church is probably an Anglo-Saxon foundation. One tradition has attributed its foundation to Aethelflaeda, Lady of the Mercians, in the early tenth century. From 1075 to 1102, it was the Cathedral Church of the Diocese of Chester. It became a parish church in the late 1540s. Part of the church fell into disuse, and now survives only as ruins. In 1881, the west tower of the church collapsed and was never rebuilt. The church's nave is a superb example of Norman architecture.

The grounds of St John's Church adjoin the **GROSVENOR PARK** on the east. Twenty acres of land were given to the City by Richard, 2nd Marquess of Westminster, in 1867. He also paid for it to be landscaped by Edward Kemp, a pupil of Joseph Paxton, architect of the Crystal Palace. A statue of the 2nd Marquess, by Thomas Thornycroft, was erected in the centre of the Park in 1869. The Shipgate, which formerly stood to the West of the Bridgegate, and an arch from the medieval St Mary's Nunnery, have been re-erected in the Park. The Park extends to the River Dee in the south; and there is a scented garden for the blind. **Grosvenor Park Lodge**, by the northern entrance, was designed by John Douglas in the 1860s. It is black and white, and decorated with statues representing the Norman earls of Chester.

Returning to the Newgate, the visitor may look west along **PEPPER STREET**, which follows the line of the south wall of the Roman fortress westwards, towards Bridge Street. It was originally the heart of St Michael's Parish. However, its eighteenth- and nineteenth-century houses were demolished in the late 1960s, and Pepper Street was widened as part of the inner ring road scheme. Much of the north side is occupied by part of the Grosvenor-Laing Shopping Precinct (**see** page 30); and in the distance can be seen the tower of St Michael's Church, now the Chester Heritage Centre (**see** page 44).

Walking south along the wall from the Newgate, the visitor looks down on **PARK STREET** to the west. A large Victorian house, which dates from 1881, is built in the 'black and white' style and bears the inscription, 'The fear of the Lord is the fountain of life'. Adjoining this house to the south, is a row of six cottages known as the **Nine Houses**, because they were originally nine in number. They have a timber-framed superstructure, on a sandstone base. This is a rare combination outside Chester. By the 1950s, they had almost fallen into ruin. However, they were restored and improved in 1968–69. Further along, on the corner of Park Street and Albion Street, is the **Albion Inn**, which retains a delightful Edwardian atmosphere. Beyond, in Albion Street, the **Volunteer Drill Hall** was built for the Chester Rifle and Artillery Volunteer Corps, which was formed in 1859. Shaped like a miniature fort, the Drill Hall was opened ten years later.

The tour continues from the Newgate south along the City walls, to **THE GROVES**. To leave the walls, visitors descend the 'Wishing Steps', which were constructed in 1785, and featured in a film of Chester made in 1933; and then the Recorder's Steps. These are named after Roger Comberbach, who served as Recorder of Chester from 1700 to 1720.

The Groves are one of Chester's most popular recreation areas. There is a pleasant promenade along the riverside, shaded by trees; and a delightful Edwardian bandstand. Regattas have been held here since the early nineteenth century; and pleasure boats ply on the river. For more than 100 years, such launches as the S.S. *Ormonde*, have taken visitors up river, for a glimpse of Eaton Hall, seat of the Duke of Westminster.

The Groves have associations with the Saxon King Harold. According to legend, he was not killed at the Battle of Hastings in 1066, but came to Chester, where he lived as a hermit in the **Anchorite's Cell**. This is a simple sandstone building to the north of the Groves. In the eighteenth century, the Weavers' Company used it as a meeting house.

At the bottom of **Souter's Lane**, which links the Newgate and the Groves, is a red brick Georgian house, which was the Palace of the Bishop of Chester, from the 1870s until 1921. It is now a Y.M.C.A. hostel.

The pleasant southern bank of the river is reached by means of an iron **Suspension Bridge**. This was first built in 1852, to link Chester with the new suburb of Queen's Park. It was rebuilt in 1923. A piece of the coiled steel used in its construction, is preserved in a paper weight in the Town Hall.

The suburb of **Queen's Park** was laid out in the 1850s by Enoch Gerrard, and many of Chester's more prosperous citizens moved to its desirable villa residences. The large neo-Georgian building erected in 1937 as the headquarters of the Army's Western Command, dominates the south bank of the river.

The Marlborough Pub

A pathway along the south bank leads to **The Meadows**, formerly known as the Earl's Eye. These were a gift to the City by Mr and Mrs H. F. Brown in 1929, on condition that they were always to be used by the citizens for recreation purposes.

Walking westwards from the Groves, the visitor will reach the **OLD DEE BRIDGE**. Here, the sense of history is very great. Until the nineteenth century, the Dee Bridge was the only bridge at Chester. It may be Roman in origin: archaeological evidence found in Lower Bridge Street indicates this. The Domesday Book, compiled in 1086, describes arrangements for the repair of a bridge in the time of King Edward the Confessor. The Chronicle of St Werburgh's Abbey records that the bridge at Chester fell down in 1227; and in 1279 it was washed away in a flood. A document of 1288 records that it was built partly in timber, and partly in stone. By the eighteenth century, the Old Dee Bridge was considered 'very narrow and dangerous'. A tower at the southern end of the bridge was demolished in the 1780s, and the bridge was widened in 1826.

The **Weir**, to the north of the Old Dee Bridge, is said to have been built by Earl Hugh I in the eleventh century, to provide water power for the Dee Mills. For many centuries, the Dee Mills were owned by the earls of Chester and the Crown, although they were purchased by the Wrench family in the late eighteenth century. In the seventeenth century, eleven water wheels were in operation. The Dee Mills were damaged by fire on several occasions: after the fire of 1819 damage was estimated at £40,000. Chester Corporation acquired the Mills in 1895, but they did not operate at a profit, and were demolished in 1910. The **Hydro Electric Power Station** was opened on the site of the Mills, in 1913.

The Old Dee Bridge links Chester and **Handbridge**. In the nineteenth century, this was a working class area. **Salmon Leap**, to the north of the Old Dee Bridge, is built on the site of a tobacco and snuff manufactory. There were several streets of small, terraced houses. Sty Lane (renamed Greenway Street in the early nineteenth century) links the road known as Handbridge with the river, and was particularly associated with the salmon fishermen. However, several fine buildings were erected in the late nineteenth century, notably the **Handbridge Institute**, at the corner of Handbridge and Eaton Road; and the **Parish Church of St Mary-without-the-Walls**. The church was completed in 1887, chiefly at the expense of the 1st Duke of Westminster. In recent years, many of the nineteenth-century houses in Handbridge, owned by the Grosvenor Estate, have been replaced by small neo-Georgian terraced houses.

Handbridge is also noted for **Edgar's Field**, given to Chester by the 1st Duke of Westminster in 1892. Legend says that King Edgar had a palace here in the tenth century. In an outcrop of sandstone rock, there is a shrine to the Roman goddess, Minerva. It is a unique Roman monument, but the image of the goddess has virtually disappeared through the ravages of weather, time, and neglect.

Chester's **Overleigh Cemetery** adjoins Edgar's Field to the west. It was designed by the architect, T. M. Penson, between 1848 and 1850. Although much of the original landscaping, including a lake, has disappeared, it remains a most attractive example of a Victorian cemetery. Notable monuments include one to Henry Raikes, Chancellor of the Diocese of Chester, from 1830 to 1854. Edward Langtry, husband of the 'Jersey Lily', is also buried there.

Returning to the Old Dee Bridge, the visitor is recommended to walk west from the Bridgegate, along Castle Drive. The **BRIDGEGATE** dates from 1782. It replaced a medieval gate, which guarded the Old Dee Bridge. A tower was built above this gate by John Tyrer in 1600, who used it to store water raised from the River Dee, which was distributed through pipes to various properties in the City.

The line of the City walls between the Bridgegate and the Grosvenor Bridge, was changed in the 1830s during extensions to Chester Castle. **County Hall**, headquarters of Cheshire County Council, is built partly on the site of the Castle Gaol. It was begun before the Second World War, but not completed until 1957. It was opened by H.M. The Queen, on 11 July that year.

A short distance from County Hall, along Castle Drive, there is an excellent view of the **GROSVENOR BRIDGE**. After considerable agitation for improved communications between Chester and North Wales, the foundation stone of the new bridge was laid by Earl Grosvenor in 1827. The Earl also donated £1000 to the building fund. The Grosvenor Bridge was designed by the architect, Thomas Harrison, who did not live to see its completion. It was opened and named by H.R.H. Princess Victoria on 17 October 1832.

The Grosvenor Bridge

The new approach road to the Grosvenor Bridge, cut through the Roodee. The much smaller, detached part to the south, known as the **Little Roodee**, is used as a car park, and occasionally as a fairground. The **ROODEE** is a feature unique to Chester. It takes its name from the rood, or cross, whose base can still be seen there; and the word 'eye', which means land partly surrounded by water. For many centuries, the citizens used it to graze their cattle; as a place of recreation; and as a training ground for soldiers. In the sixteenth century, the football match between the Shoemakers and Drapers Companies began at the Cross on the Roodee. Football violence caused the City Assembly to ban the match in 1540. It was replaced firstly by footraces, and later by horse races. Chester Racecourse on the Roodee, is therefore one of the oldest in the country. The main meeting is held every May: its richest prize, the Chester Cup, originated in the Chester Tradesmen's Plate, which was first run in 1824. The first grandstand on the Roodee was built in 1817, to provide accommodation for the gentry attending the races. The foundation stone of the present grandstand, was laid by the Duke of Westminster in 1899.

From Grosvenor Bridge, the visitor should continue his tour by walking north up **Grosvenor Road**, to the massive entrance gateway of **CHESTER CASTLE**. Chester Castle was rebuilt between 1788 and 1822, to the designs of Thomas Harrison, one of the leading architects of the Greek Revival. It has a central block, with two separate wings at right angles to it, surrounding a massive parade ground. The statue of Queen Victoria was unveiled in 1903. The Regimental Museum of the Cheshire Regiment is housed in the northern block. The Duke of Norfolk's Regiment was raised in 1689. It became known as the 22nd Regiment of Foot, and, after Army reforms in the 1870s, as the Cheshire Regiment. H.R.H. The Prince of Wales is Colonel in Chief of the Regiment.

Very little evidence of the medieval castle remains. Agricola's Tower, at the south-east corner of the central block, dates from the late twelfth or early thirteenth century. It contains the Chapel of St Mary de Castro. The gaol at Chester Castle was visited by the prison reformer, John Howard, at the end of the eighteenth century. He compared it with the Black Hole of Calcutta. The gaol was closed in 1877, and part of its site is now occupied by County Hall.

Opposite the entrance to Chester Castle, a rectangular building of glass and concrete, houses the headquarters of the Cheshire Constabulary. It was designed by the County Architect, Edgar Taberner, and opened in 1967. It occupies the site of St Mary's Priory of Benedictine Nuns, founded in the twelfth century.

A statue of Stapleton Cotton, 1st Viscount Combermere, who fought in the French and Napoleonic Wars, stands in the middle of the road between the Police Headquarters and the castle entrance. It was executed by Baron Marochetti in the late 1860s.

Grosvenor Road roundabout stands on the site of **St Bridget's Church**. Another of Chester's ancient parish churches, this originally stood opposite St Michael's in Bridge Street. It was demolished in 1828, to make way for Grosvenor Street. Rebuilt in an elegant classical style, at the southern end of

Chester Races

Grosvenor Street, it survived only until 1892. However, some of its gravestones remain in place. An obelisk on the south side of the roundabout, commemorates the Presbyterian minister, Matthew Henry.

On the east side of Grosvenor Street, are the **Trustee Savings Bank**, and Chester's Grosvenor Museum. The Chester Savings Bank was founded in 1817. Its building, with Perpendicular windows, and a clock tower, was designed by James Harrison, and opened in 1853.

The **GROSVENOR MUSEUM** in Grosvenor Street contains exceptionally fine collections for a provincial museum. Its exhibitions illustrate the Archaeology, Natural History, and Local History of Chester and the surrounding region.

Since Chester was an important military site, particular prominence is given to the two galleries which deal with this period. The Newstead Gallery describes the fortress by means of models, illustrations, and dioramas, in addition to displaying objects recovered by excavation. An adjacent gallery

39

St Mary's Hill

contains an unrivalled collection of inscribed material, mainly tombstones. Archaeological excavations in Chester District are organised by the Field Section of the Grosvenor Museum.

The Museum has a considerable collection of paintings, watercolours, prints, and drawings connected with the City of Chester. It is particularly known for its watercolours by Louise Rayner; and the works of other local artists such as Moses Griffiths and William Tasker.

There is also an outstanding collection of silver, which includes the Civic Plate with important pieces dating from the immediate post Civil War period. In addition, there is a collection of silver made and assayed in Chester.

From time to time, the Museum displays part of its extensive coin collection, which is particularly strong in coins minted in Chester during Saxon and Norman times; and also during the Civil War and the great Recoinage of William III.

The Museum also contains collections connected with traditional trades

St Mary's Centre

and crafts. A recent addition to the collection is a Dee salmon boat, specially built for the Museum by a local boatyard, in 1980–81.

A publications list of the books, pamphlets, slides, maps, and postcards on sale, is available from the Publications and Enquiry counter in the Museum. An Educational Service provides information and teaching facilities for groups visiting the Museum. Further information about the Museum's collections and services may be obtained from the Curator.

After visiting the Museum, the visitor is directed to retrace his steps to the Grosvenor roundabout, walk a short way east along Castle Street, and turn into **ST MARY'S HILL**. This is a steep, cobbled street of great charm. It links Castle Street with Shipgate Street and Lower Bridge Street. At the top of the street, modern flats and maisonnettes blend successfully into their Victorian surroundings. **St Mary's School** adjoining them to the south, was opened in 1846; and **St Mary's Rectory**, lower down the hill, is an early nineteenth-century house, built in the Tudor style.

To the west of St Mary's Hill, is **St Mary's Church**, formerly the focal point of the Parish of St Mary on the Hill. It was extensively restored by James Harrison in the early 1860s. It contains fine monuments notably those of Thomas Gamull, and Philip Oldfield, who both died in 1613. Like St Michael's Church, St Mary's was declared redundant in 1972. It was acquired by Cheshire County Council, and has become **St Mary's Centre**, which is used mainly for educational purposes.

When the visitor arrives at the bottom of St Mary's Hill, he is recommended to begin the long climb up Lower Bridge Street and Bridge Street, to St Peter's Church and the Cross, at the heart of the City. **LOWER BRIDGE STREET** ceased to be a principal thoroughfare when Grosvenor Street was built in the 1820s. However, there are many buildings which indicate its former status. Commencing at the Bridgegate, on the west side of the street, and walking north, the visitor will pass the '**Bear and Billet**'. This is a black and white, 'tiered' building, which dates from 1664. It was once a town house of the earls of Shrewsbury. The **Three Kings Studio**, which adjoins the 'Bear and Billet' to the north, has an eighteenth-century façade which conceals a timber-framed building containing a cruck beam. **Gamul House and Terrace** also has an eighteenth- or early nineteenth-century façade, which conceals timber framing. Gamul House was the town house of the Gamull family; and Charles I stayed there in 1645 as the guest of Sir Francis Gamull, who had been Mayor of Chester in 1634–35. Gamul House and Terrace and **Gamul Place** at their rear, are a superb example of the City's Conservation programme. In Gamul Place, nineteenth-century terraced cottages have been restored and modernised. The flats and maisonnettes which front St Mary's Hill, form the western side of Gamul Place, although in an elevated position. A pleasant walkway leads from Gamul Place to the top of Castle Street. This area was visited by H.R.H. The Duke of Gloucester, during European Architectural Heritage Year, 1975.

North of Gamul House, '**Ye Olde King's Head**' stands on the corner of Lower Bridge Street and Castle Street. In the seventeenth and early eighteenth centuries it was the home of the Randle Holmes of Chester. Four members of the family were antiquarians and herald painters; and Randle Holme II made the first attempt at organising the City Archives. 'Ye Olde King's Head' was restored in 1934 and 1968.

The area between 'Ye Olde King's Head' and the top of Lower Bridge Street was formerly neglected, but is now undergoing comprehensive restoration. A nineteenth-century façade has been preserved to provide a frontage which is in keeping with the street scene. One good example of Georgian architecture should be noted: the **Oddfellows' Hall** or Bridge House. This was built for John Williams, a prominent lawyer, in the early eighteenth century. Chester College occupied this building for a short time after the College was founded in 1839. In addition, '**The Falcon**', at the corner of Lower Bridge Street and Grosvenor Street, was re-opened as an inn in 1982, following a major programme of restoration. This is a seventeenth-century timber-framed building, once the town house of the Grosvenor family. In 1643, Richard Grosvenor petitioned the

City Assembly for permission to enlarge this house, by enclosing the Row beneath it. He was employed in the King's garrison, and claimed that the house was far too little to receive him and his family.

There are also interesting buildings on the east side of Lower Bridge Street. **Bridge Place** near the Bridgegate, is an elegant range of eighteenth-century houses. There is also **St Olave's Church**, on the corner of Lower Bridge Street, and St Olave Street, which dates from the twelfth century. It is a small, sandstone building, which James Harrison restored in the 1850s. The building to its east, was once occupied by St Olave's Ragged School, founded in 1852, an indication of the poverty of this area. It was succeeded by an elementary school, which closed in 1941.

To the north of St Olave Street, there is a large Georgian building, with an impressive portico. This was built as Park House in 1715, but it later became the fashionable **Albion Hotel**. The Duke of Wellington stayed there in 1820. North of the Albion Hotel, there is **Tudor House**, which has claimed, though without supporting evidence, to be the oldest house in Chester.

There were once Rows in Lower Bridge Street, and a few traces survive there, but they are best seen in their fully developed form in three of the main streets of the City: Bridge Street, Eastgate Street, and Watergate Street. **THE ROWS** are unique to Chester. They consist of covered galleries above the shops at street level; and are reached by steps from the streets. Each section of Row has a 'stall' where goods are often displayed; and people stand to watch the street scene below. The origin of the Rows has never been explained in a satisfactory way. One theory advocates a gradual development. Another theory claims that the Rows were built as a town planning exercise after the fire of 1278, which destroyed most of Chester. Documentary evidence, however, supports a gradual development which lasted from the thirteenth until the eighteenth century. The three elements which influenced the form of the Rows, were all in existence by the middle fourteenth century: 'seldae' or stalls at street level; cellars; and the Rows themselves. The first references to 'seldae' occur in the thirteenth century. Some were possibly temporary structures, others seem to have been structures built in stone. Cellars, similar to those in Bridge Street, Eastgate Street, and Watergate Street, are first mentioned in fourteenth-century records. The first references to Rows, occur in a Portmote Court Roll of the City of Chester, dated 1327–30. Their elevated position is confirmed by a Grant of 1356. Documentary evidence of the sixteenth and seventeenth century indicates that buildings were erected which overhung the Rows and Streets. For example, a Conveyance of 1592 describes 'Chambers and forefrontes right over the same Shopps . . .' in Eastgate Street. Next, posts were erected to support the overhang. Finally, the vacant space created by the posts at street level, was filled in. As late as 1706, Martha Rickmore, widow, asked permission to build a small shop on a small piece of ground in Bridge Street, 'under a shop in the Row . . .' This filling in therefore created the stalls in the Rows, which Cestrians and visitors today use as vantage points.

Over the centuries, many Rows disappeared, but by the eighteenth century, the tradition was strong enough to survive rebuilding both in timber and stone.

BRIDGE STREET was the Roman Via Praetoria. Walking north, the visitor retraces the footsteps of the Romans from the south gate of the fortress, to the Principia or headquarters building. There are many styles of architecture. **Owen Owen's** department store, on the west side of the street, incorporates three medieval arches at Row level. The building is known as the 'Three Old Arches'. The '**Dutch Houses**', so called because they are said to resemble a Dutch style of architecture, date from the seventeenth century. They may be recognised by their twisted pillars. The 'Dutch Houses', including a fine seventeenth-century plaster ceiling, were restored in the 1970s. The '**Plane Tree**', which adjoins the Dutch Houses to the north, was built by T. M. Lockwood in the 1870s. **No. 12 Bridge Street**, occupied by Bookland, incorporates a medieval crypt, which is thought to date from about 1270–80.

On the east side of Bridge Street, at the corner of Pepper Street, is **St Michael's Church**, now **CHESTER HERITAGE CENTRE**. St Michael's was one of Chester's smaller parish churches; and it was first mentioned in a charter issued to Norton Priory by Henry II about 1154–60. Few of the church's medieval features survive. However, the north aisle, built in the Perpendicular style of church architecture, dates from the late fourteenth or early fifteenth century; and the beautifully decorated chancel roof dates from about 1496. A plaque on the south wall, records that the east end of the church was enlarged in 1679. A wooden steeple was replaced by a stone tower in 1710; and between 1849 and 1851, St Michael's Church was almost completely rebuilt to the designs of the Chester architect, James Harrison, 'the other Harrison of Chester'. He chose, not the traditional local red sandstone, but a more durable type of this stone.

The depopulation of the City centre caused St Michael's congregation to dwindle, and the church was declared redundant in 1972. It reopened in 1975 as the **Chester Heritage Centre**. This was Britain's first Architectural Heritage Centre. In 1966, reports on the historic towns of Bath, Chester, Chichester, and York had been commissioned jointly by the Minister of Housing and Local Government, and the City and County Councils concerned. **Chester: A Study in Conservation**, prepared by Donald W. Insall and Associates, was published in 1968. In the following year, Chester City Council designated the whole of the walled City and some areas adjacent, a Conservation area. This area covers 200 acres, and contains over 600 buildings considered to be of 'Special Architectural or Historic Interest'. A Conservation Officer was appointed in 1971, to liaise between the City Council, owners of property, architects, and contractors. A Conservation fund was established; and Donald W. Insall and Associates were appointed consultant architects.

In 1975, Chester was one of the four United Kingdom 'pilot projects' in European Architectural Heritage Year. To celebrate Chester's achievements in Conservation, St Michael's Church was purchased from the Church

Commissioners. With financial help from the Department of the Environment, it was converted into a Heritage Centre, which was opened by H.R.H. The Duke of Gloucester on 25 June 1975.

The Heritage Centre contains a small theatre, where an audio-visual presentation gives a vivid description of Chester's history and buildings. In addition, permanent and temporary exhibitions describe the City's Conservation programme; and inform the public of progress being made in securing the preservation of the past.

Since a change of policy in March 1980, the Chester Heritage Centre has encompassed all aspects of the City's heritage. A programme of special temporary exhibitions, on historic and archaeological, as well as architectural themes, is drawn up each year; schools are encouraged to visit the Heritage Centre; and St Michael's has become a lively meeting place, as well as an exhibition centre.

After leaving the Heritage Centre, the visitor should turn north up Bridge Street. On the east side, **No. 55 Bridge Street** is an ornate Victorian black and white building, decorated with a statue of Charles I. Further north, **No. 47 Bridge Street Row**, which dates from the seventeenth century, was used as St Michael's Rectory. It was restored in 1974–75. The most impressive building on this side of the street, is probably the massive entrance to **St Michael's Arcade**. This was built in 1910 in the Baroque style, with white tiles. There was a public outcry, and the 2nd Duke of Westminster, who owned the site, ordered it to be demolished, and replaced by the present black and white structure.

THE CROSS has great significance for Chester's history. **The High Cross** where merchants made bargains, stood on this site from 1407 until the English Civil War. After a sojourn in the Roman Gardens adjoining the Newgate, it was re-erected in the centre of the City, in 1975. For many centuries, the Cross was the centre of City government. The Mayor, Aldermen, and Common Councilmen met in the Pentice, originally a timber-framed structure, built against the south side of St Peter's Church. From the Pentice, they watched performances of the Mystery Plays; the defeat of the Spanish Armada in 1588 was celebrated by firing a cannon outside the Pentice; and when Charles II's charter was brought to Chester in 1685, the conduit, or water cistern, at the Pentice was filled with wine. It was also a scene of riot and disturbance. Master weavers and their journeymen fought at the Cross in 1399; and during the 1732 election the Pentice was stormed by an angry mob. Because of traffic congestion at the Cross the Pentice was demolished in 1803, and City government moved to the Exchange in Northgate Street (**see** page 18).

ST PETER'S CHURCH at the Cross was probably an Anglo-Saxon foundation. Although it was restored in 1886–87, its interior dates from the fourteenth or fifteenth century. It is unusual in not having a nave, and is almost square in shape. Monumental brasses are rare in West Cheshire. One, badly worn, in St Peter's Church is said to be that of a fifteenth-century lawyer. St Peter's is the church used by the Freemen and Guilds of Chester for their services.

The Rows, Watergate Street

Other buildings at the Cross are mostly Victorian. The ornate half-timbered building on the corner of Bridge Street and Eastgate Street, and its larger neighbour in Eastgate Street, date from 1888, and were designed by T. M. Lockwood. The building at the corner of Bridge Street and Watergate Street is also Lockwood. This is an interesting mixture of timber and brick, and dates from 1892.

From the Cross, the tour proceeds westward along **WATERGATE STREET**, which slopes gently to the Watergate. Nineteenth-century prints show that it was a busy street, and markets were held in Watergate Row until the public market opened in 1863. Since 1966, Watergate Street has been divided by the inner ring road.

Walking westward from the Cross, on the south side of the street, the visitor will first see **God's Providence House**. The date 1652 inscribed on the building, and the inscription 'God's Providence is Mine Inheritance' celebrates the legend that the house's inhabitants were spared by the plague. There were plans to demolish God's Providence House in the 1860s. The Chester Archaeological Society protested, and the house's reconstruction was supervised by James Harrison. The wine and spirit business of **Quellyn Roberts** adjoins God's Providence House to the west. Their premises incorporate the largest medieval crypt in Chester, which probably dates from the late thirteenth century. The **Leche House** is named after the Leche family of Carden, who claimed descent from John Leche, surgeon to Edward III. This house has associations with Catherine of Aragon. Pomegranates, the symbol of Aragon, are represented in its ornate plaster work. Catherine's first husband was Arthur, Prince of Wales, who paid a state visit to Chester in 1499. There is also a gallery with a 'squint hole' concealed by a Spanish grille. Further west, **Bishop Lloyd's House** was restored by Chester City Council in 1973–76. It has associations with the United States. It is named after George Lloyd, Bishop of Sodor and Man, 1599–1605, and Bishop of Chester, 1605–15. His daughter, Anne, married first Thomas, son of David Yale, Chancellor of the Diocese of Chester; and secondly, Theophilus Eaton, founder of the settlement at New Haven, Connecticut. Anne's grandson, Elihu Yale, came to Chester as a young man, and served an apprenticeship to Alderman Gawen Hudson. In 1669, he was fined £20 by Chester City Quarter Sessions, for spreading scurrilous stories about Mrs Hudson. Bishop Lloyd's House is ornately carved. Carvings include the Legs of Man; the Arms of James I; and a variety of heraldic beasts.

The north side of Watergate Street is dominated by the Georgian elegance of **Booth Mansion**. This was a fashionable Assembly Room in the eighteenth century, but it gradually fell into decay. A programme of restoration was undertaken, and Booth Mansion opened in July 1980, as the Chester Branch of the London firm of Sotheby.

Trinity Church stands on the north-eastern corner of Watergate Street, and the inner ring road. Another of Chester's medieval churches, it was rebuilt by James Harrison in the 1860s. It was declared redundant in 1961. Trinity Church has served the densely populated area between Watergate Street and

Princess Street, at the rear of the Town Hall. Most of this property was demolished in the 1930s. In 1963, Trinity Church became the **GUILDHALL** of the Freemen and Guilds of the City of Chester. Twenty-three companies are represented there; and the Guilds retain much of their medieval ceremonial. The **Custom House** of the Port of Chester, which dates from 1869, is built into an angle of the church.

The 'detached' part of Watergate Street slopes sharply to the Watergate. On the southern side of the street, the visitor will see **Stanley Palace**, which is said to have been built by Peter Warburton in 1591. It passed to the Stanley family of Alderley in the seventeenth century. The Earl of Derby acquired it in 1899, and assigned it, on a long lease, to Chester City Council, in 1928. Stanley Palace was restored by the City Council in the 1930s. **Watergate House**, to its west, is a large classical building built by Thomas Harrison in 1820 for Henry Potts, Clerk of the Peace for Cheshire. It has an unusual circular hall; and it featured in the television serial, 'The House of Caradus'.

On the opposite side of the street, **No. 104 Watergate Flags** housed the Queen's School from 1878 until its new premises were opened in 1883. This house, on the corner of Watergate Street and City Walls Road, also has a rare Sedan Chair Porch. The Porch was restored in 1981.

In the Middle Ages, the River Dee was closed to the **WATERGATE**. Ships unloaded their cargoes there, which were bought into Chester through this gate. The present Watergate, with its round arch, was built in 1788.

The tour continues northwards from the Watergate, past Stanley Place, the Queen's School, and the Royal Infirmary, to Bonewaldesthorne's Tower. **Stanley Place** has two terraces of elegant Georgian houses, built in the 1780s. To the east (of Stanley Place), between Stanley Place and the inner ring road, are the stables owned by the Chester Race Company. The **Queen's School** was founded, with the support of the 1st Duke of Westminster, to educate the daughters of the middle classes. The Duke obtained Queen Victoria's permission for the school's name, in 1882. The buildings were designed by the architect E. A. Ould, a pupil of John Douglas. The Queen's School occupies the site of the City Gaol, opened in 1808, and closed in 1872. It was a large rectangular building. Its western entrance faced the City walls; and the populace gathered on the walls to watch public executions.

The **Royal Infirmary** adjoins the Queen's School to the north. The eighteenth century has been described as the Age of Philanthropy, and the Infirmary was founded, with the help of a bequest from William Stratford, in 1755. It was opened in the Bluecoat Hospital, but moved to a purpose-built hospital, facing the City walls, in 1761. The Infirmary was supported by subscribers, who had the right to recommend patients for treatment. The Infirmary became a pioneer in several fields: Dr John Haygarth conducted a census of the outbreak of disease in Chester in 1774, and advocated the isolation of fever patients. Dr Griffith Rowlands organised the training of midwives in the early nineteenth century. The title 'Royal' was conferred on the Infirmary by George V, when he opened the Albert Wood Wings in 1914.

Bishop Lloyds Palace

Stanley Palace, Stanley Place

Bonewaldesthorne's Tower is a short step north along the City walls from the Infirmary. A spur wall, about 100 feet in length, connects Bonewaldesthorne's Tower with the **Water Tower**, which was built to protect the Port of Chester. The contract for the building of the Water Tower is dated 1322–23. Its architect was John de Helpeston, who was promised £100. In the 1830s, the Water Tower became the Museum of the Mechanics' Insititution. Today, the Grosvenor Museum operates the Water Tower as a branch museum.

From these towers, there is a splendid view of canal and railway. A staircase of three locks, to the north of the City walls, lowers the Chester Canal, opened in 1779, almost to the level of the River Dee. There is also a connection with the Ellesmere Canal, opened in 1796, which links Chester and Ellesmere Port. **Tarvin House**, in Tower Road, was first the Canal Hotel, and later the offices of the Canal Company. From 1970 to 1974, it was the headquarters of Tarvin Rural District Council, and it is now occupied by the Environmental Health Department of Chester City Council. The railway line, which breaches the City walls, links Chester and North Wales.

From Bonewaldesthorne's Tower, the visitor should continue east towards the Northgate **Pemberton's Parlour**, also known as the Goblin Tower, is named after a ropemaker who worked there. On the Parlour, there are two cartouches, carved by the sculptor, John Tilston, and a tablet recording the names of the Mayors and the Murengers, between 1702 and 1708. The Murengers were the officers responsible for the upkeep of the walls. East of Pemberton's Parlour is **St Martin's Gate**, built in 1966 after a section of the City wall had been destroyed, prior to the building of the inner ring road. Between St Martin's Gate and the Northgate, is **Morgan's Mount**, named after the commander of a gun battery, which was place on this tower during the Siege of Chester, 1644–46. The northern section of the walls was heavily bombarded by the Parliamentary forces.

From this section of the City wall, there is an excellent view of the **Bluecoat School**, built in 1717 to house a charity school which had been founded by Bishop Nicholas Stratford in 1700, to combat the growth of vice and debauchery in Chester. A statue of a Bluecoat boy stands over the entrance. The school closed in 1949. The southern wing of the Bluecoat School was occupied by the Chapel of Little St John. It was linked to the gaol in the Northgate by the Bridge of Sighs, built in 1793. The foundation of the Almshouses at the rear of the Bluecoat School, is ascribed to Earl Ranulph III of Chester. The Almshouses were rebuilt in 1854.

The final part of the tour returns the visitor from the Northgate, along Northgate Street to the Town Hall. The **NORTHGATE** is a severe classical arch, designed by Thomas Harrison, and built in 1808–10. It was commissioned by Earl Grosvenor, when he was Mayor in 1807–08. The Earl objected to the original design, which was similar to the Watergate. The City Council accepted his objections, when he offered to erect the gate at his own expense. The old Northgate, which was demolished, housed the City Gaol. It was in the charge of the Sheriffs, who also received the toll at this gate.

NORTHGATE STREET was the Roman **Via Decumana**. The barrack blocks of the fortress were near its north gate. The modern office block to the south of the Northgate, has therefore been named **Centurion House**. It partly occupies the site of the Northgate Brewery, closed in 1969, which in its turn had incorporated the Golden Falcon Inn, where George Frederick Handel, composer of 'The Messiah', is said to have stayed in 1741. To the south of Centurion House, is the site of the old **City Fire Station**. It was a tall black and white building, built in 1911, for the Earl of Chester's Volunteer Fire Brigade. From 1836 to 1863, the Chester Police were also firemen, but they demonstrated their inefficiency when the Exchange burnt down in 1862. In the following year, the citizens formed a Volunteer Fire Brigade, although the superintendent's wages were paid by the City Council. The Brigade came under Council control in 1914. The Fire Station became redundant when new premises were opened in St Anne Street, by H.R.H. The Prince of Wales, in 1971. Although the old Fire Station has been demolished, its façade has been preserved. The former '**Blue Bell**' Inn, to the south of the Fire Station, dates from the fifteenth century.

The visitor should pause to admire **King Street**. It slopes gently from Northgate Street towards the inner ring road; and contains houses dating from the eighteenth and nineteenth centuries. An extensive programme of restoration, has in recent years, revitalised King Street, and made it a highly desirable residential area.

The '**Pied Bull**', on the corner of King Street and Northgate Street, is one of Chester's oldest inns. It has an eighteenth-century façade, but much earlier features within. It was also a coaching inn. A tablet records distances between Chester and London, and other places served by the coaching system. George Borrow may have stayed at the 'Pied Bull', when he visited Chester in 1854. In *Wild Wales*, he made derogatory remarks about Chester Ale and Cheshire Cheese. The Town Hall, starting point of the tour, is a short distance south of the 'Pied Bull'.

It may seem to the visitor that there are omissions from the tour, but of necessity, it has been selective. Every building in the centre of Chester, or its site, has a recorded history, often dating back to the Middle Ages. The City Archivist invites readers who wish to check the information given in the text, or to discover more about Chester's history, to consult those sources in the Chester City Records Office which she has used in compiling this account of a City which 'teems with historical associations, and is virtually a museum full of interest to the historian and antiquary'.

ANTIQUI DIERUM
COLANT ANTIQUUM

52

THE ARMORIAL BEARINGS OF THE CHESTER CITY COUNCIL

BY THE PROVISIONS of the Local Government Act of 1972, it was not possible for the new City Council to inherit the former City Arms as they stood because of the addition of the large rural districts of Chester and Tarvin. In view, however, of the antiquity, historical associations, and beauty of the former sixteenth-century Arms, the Kings of Arms agreed to re-grant them with suitable additions relative to the enlarged area. The new Arms, therefore, preserve the old Arms without disturbance of their original pattern, but with what may be considered as 'honourable augmentations' which make them representative of the whole new area.

*The **Shield** is the ancient combination of the Arms of England and of the Earldom of Chester, three gold lions on red halved with three gold wheat-sheaves on blue, to which has been added a gold border charged with eight acorns, referring to the rural areas surrounding the City. These were formerly wholly covered with oak forest, much of which still stands.*

*The **Crest** features the sword of the former City Crest entwined with two branches of oak, representing the three former areas now bound together in the new City.*

*The **Supporters** are those of the former City, the gold lion of England and the white wolf of Hugh Lupus, first Norman Earl of Chester, with crowns about their neck. To these have been added pendants in the form of red castles referring to the historic strongholds of the rural areas, including the royal castles at Chester, Shotwick, and Beeston.*

*The **Badge** is a variation of the former one, and features Hugh Lupus' wolf's head on a background of the red and blue of the shield in a pattern suggesting the City walls, all enclosed in a wreath of oak, and again representing the old City surrounded by the rural areas.*

*The **Motto** is that inscribed on the former City's Patent of Arms of 1580 and used as the motto to its Arms ever since: Antiqui Colant Antiquum Dierum: 'Let the Ancients worship the Ancient of Days'.*

The additions to the former Arms were suggested by the City of Chester's honorary heraldic advisors, H. Ellis Tomlinson, M.A., F.H.S. and T. Alan Keith-Hill, F.R.S.A., F.S.A.(SCOT). They were approved in the summer of 1975 and the new Arms are officially blazoned as follows:

Arms: *Gules three lions passant guardant in pale Or, dimidiating Azure three garbs Or, all within a bordure Or charged with eight acorns proper.*

Crest: *On a wreath Or, Gules and Azure, between two branches of oak fructed proper a sword erect hilt and pommel Or, within a sheath Sable garnished Or, encircled with a sword belt sable buckled and garnished Or entwined with the oak. Mantled to the dexter Gules, and to the sinister Azure, doubled Argent.*

Supporters: *On the dexter side a lion Or gorged with a coronet Argent, pendent therefrom a castle of three towers Gules and on the sinister side a wolf Argent gorged with a coronet Or, pendent therefrom a like castle.*

Badge: *On a roundel per fess embattled Azure and Gules environed of a garland of oak fructed proper a wolf's head erased Argent armed and langued Or.*

The Armorial Bearings of the Chester City Council must not be reproduced without the written approval of the City Council.

THE CATHEDRAL

Hours of Service:
Weekdays: 7.45 a.m., 10 a.m., 5.15 p.m. (Sung Tuesdays and Thursdays).
Saturdays: 7.45 a.m., 10 a.m., 4.15 p.m. (Sung).
Sundays: 7.45 a.m., 10.30 a.m., 11.30 a.m. (Sung), 3.30 p.m. (Sung), 6.30 p.m.
Thursdays: 1.10–7 p.m. Organ recital.

The Cathedral is open daily until 6 p.m. (winter), 7 p.m. (summer).

(The Holy Communion is celebrated in all the different chapels and particulars of these and other special services can be seen in the weekly schemes on the Cathedral notice boards or can be obtained by application to the Head Verger.)

A church or minster was founded on this site in the early tenth century, as a resting place for the body of St Werburgh (who died between 700 and 707), a Mercian princess, and a pioneer in the founding of monasteries in the northern midlands. Her shrine became the pilgrimage centre of the Abbey in the Middle Ages. The church was dedicated to St Werburgh and staffed by secular canons. The earliest document referring to the church dates from 958. Both the church and canons are mentioned in the Domesday Book. In 1093 the Norman Earl of Chester, Hugh Lupus, with the aid of St Anselm, changed the foundation to an abbey of Benedictine monks. For five centuries the building remained a monastery with widespread lands and great power, and it was not until after its dissolution in 1540 that it was made a cathedral and seat of a bishop, and the dedication was changed to Christ and the Blessed Virgin. The visitor should remember that it was designed as an abbey church and that in the buildings grouped around its cloisters he has an unrivalled opportunity to appreciate the manner of life and surroundings of the monks. Excellent guide books are provided in the Cathedral for those who wish to know more about it, but for those who have little time to spare, the following are some of its principal features in the order in which they would be seen by a visitor entering the south-west porch in St Werburgh Street. If entering at the south porch, visitors should commence at the Consistory Court. (The numbers in brackets correspond with the numbers on the Plan of the Cathedral at page 55.)

The porch, and south-west tower adjoining it, were built just before the dissolution of the Abbey, the tower still remained unfinished and only one storey high. Within the tower is the **Consistory Court** (1) with a screen and woodwork dating from 1636. In crossing to the north-west corner of the Cathedral the visitor has a fine view of the nave, begun in the fourteenth century but not completed until a century and a half later. The great arches of the **Baptistery** (2) are twelfth-century work, and enclose a font brought from

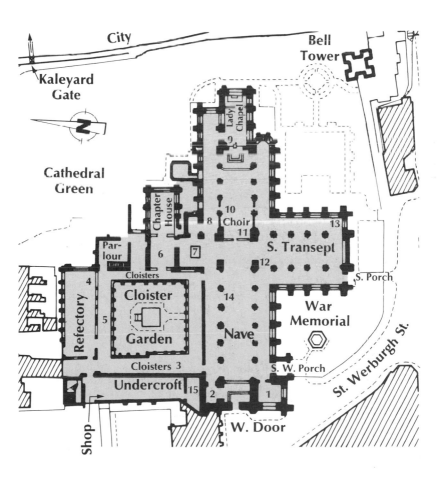

City

Kaleyard
Gate

Bell
Tower

N

Cathedral
Green

Lady Chapel

9

Chapter House

8

10 Choir

11

13

S. Transept

Parlour

6

7

12

Cloisters

4

Cloister

Garden

Refectory

5

S. Porch

14

War
Memorial

Nave

Cloisters 3

S. W. Porch

Undercroft 15

2

1

St. Werburgh St.

Shop

W. Door

Italy in 1885. A doorway at the west end of the north aisle leads to the **Cloisters** (3), where the monks studied in the arched recesses or 'carrels'. On the west side of the cloisters is the twelfth-century Norman **Undercroft** with groined vault and squat pillars; at the north end is the Cathedral Shop, open daily from 9.30, except on Sundays, and on the north side the thirteenth-century **Refectory** (4) or Dining Hall with its beautiful stone wall-pulpit from which a monk reads to the brethren during meals.

The fine hammer-beam roof, designed by F. H. Crossley of Chester, was built in 1939. Outside the Refectory door are the recesses where the monks washed their hands before dining (5). At the north-east corner of the cloisters is a vaulted room known as the parlour, now used as the choir vestry, and on the east side a doorway leads to the vestibule of the thirteenth-century **Chapter House** (6) containing part of the Cathedral's library and a cupboard with remarkably fine ironwork that is almost as old as the Chapter House itself. The Cathedral is re-entered by way of the **North Transept** with its late eleventh-century arch and the modern tomb of the seventeenth-century Bishop Pearson (7) described as 'the greatest divine of his age'. In the **North Aisle** of the Choir (8) are fragments of the twelfth-century abbey church re-used in the foundations of the present choir, built some 200 years later. The **Lady Chapel** (9) contains part of the stone shrine which once held the relics of St Werburgh, an object of pilgrimage in the Middle Ages. The **Choir** itself is famous for its late fourteenth-century stalls with their intricate carvings (10), including a Tree of Jesse (11) showing the genealogy of Christ. The great **South Transept** was added to the Cathedral in the fourteenth century and once formed the Parish Church of St Oswald. It contains many interesting memorials, including the Battle ensigns of H.M.S. *Chester* (12) the ship on which the boy Jack Cornwell won the V.C. at the Battle of Jutland, and the Colours of the Cheshire Regiment (13) along the south wall. A grotesque figure known as the Chester Imp (14) may be seen in the north clerestory of the nave, in the second bay from the east.

An audio-visual introduction to the Cathedral is shown hourly in the twelfth-century Abbots Passageway (15), entrance from the cloisters.

Light lunches and refreshments are available in the **Refectory** (4) from 10.30 a.m.–5 p.m. daily, except Sunday, from May to October.

The Bell Tower

In the south-east corner of the Cathedral precincts by the Cheshire Regiment Memorial Garden, is a free-standing tower or campanile where the Cathedral bells are hung. The tower itself is a concrete structure, with brick in-filling and clad with Bethesda slates. It was designed by George Pace and finished in 1974; and is the first free-standing Bell Tower built for a cathedral since the fifteenth century. The bells consist of a ring of twelve and a flat sixth. Each bell is named after a saint, Celtic or Anglo-Saxon, venerated in Chester and its neighbourhood. The great Tenor Bell is named after Christ and Our Lady, to whom the Cathedral is dedicated. It weighs $24\frac{3}{4}$ hundredweights, and is 4 feet 4 inches in diameter.

Mercia Square with the Cathedral in the background

CHESTER TODAY

Although no longer a port, **CHESTER** today is a thriving, modern city with plenty to offer Cestrians and the visitor, whether on business or pleasure.

Chester – Conference City

CHESTER is ideally situated and easily accessible from London (via M1, M6, M56, M53 (3 hours or $2\frac{1}{4}$ hours by train); Manchester Airport (via M56, M53 to the City centre, is $\frac{1}{2}$ hour by road); Liverpool ($\frac{1}{2}$ hour); or East Coast Ports – Harwich (241 miles); Newcastle, M62 (195 miles). It is also convenient for sailings to and from Ireland.

CHESTER is ideal for the small and medium-sized conference. A brochure featuring conference facilities, together with advice on attractive leisure programmes for delegates and their wives, is available from **Chester Marketing Bureau Ltd**, Chester Visitor Centre, Vicars Lane, Chester. Tel: (0244) 313126.

Chester – Tourist City

CHESTER is one of the most popular cities, providing facilities for tourists all year round. Short-break holidays are available during the autumn, winter and spring periods. Tourist information and an Accommodation Booking Service are available from the Chester Visitor Centre, and the Tourist Information Centre.

The **Chester Visitor Centre** is situated at Vicars Lane and the **Tourist Information Centre** is at the foot of the Town Hall steps.

The Chester Visitor Centre and the Tourist Information Centre sell film, maps, posters, the Official Guide, British Tourist Authority and English Tourist Board literature and *Where to Stay* guides, souvenirs, tickets for attractions and events and, most important, hotel and guest house reservations.

Guided Tours of the City leave from the Tourist Information Centre and the Chester Visitor Centre. The Chester guides have all attended an extensive course of lectures, have passed a written and oral examination and wear an official badge. Guided tours in most languages are available by prior arrangement with the tours booking officer, Chester Marketing Bureau. Themed walks include the Roman Soldier Wall Patrol (in full uniform) and, new in 1985, a Tudor Trail escorted by 'Eleanor Aldersey', who lived in Chester in 1573, in Tudor costume.

Apart from picturesque river and horse-drawn canal cruises, Chester's canal offers holiday facilities for those who like to relax on a leisurely holiday with their own boat. Several caravan and camping sites are available in the vicinity for those who enjoy a caravan holiday.

Shopping in the Rows

Chester – Capital Style Shopping

CHESTER is well known as a popular shopping centre. The excellence and variety of the shops, especially in the unique Rows where one can enjoy shopping under cover come rain or shine, is worthy of a city many times the size of Chester. Modern shopping precincts are also to be found in the City. The Grosvenor Precinct can be entered from Eastgate Street by the Chester Grosvenor Hotel, or from the walls via St John Street or the St Michael's Arcade.

Cow Lane Bridge/Queen Street is another shopping area, while by the Town Hall is the Forum Shopping Complex offering a wide variety of shops. Leading from the Forum and behind the Town Hall is the public market which sells the finest Cheshire produce. Banks, garages, parking grounds and comfortable restaurants are all conveniently situated. There is six-day trading but some shops and the market close on Wednesday.

Chester – Enterprise City

CHESTER, until medieval times the most important port on the north-west coast, a thriving commercial centre in Victorian times, today offers splendid opportunities, including scope for specialised light industries. The **Chester Enterprise Centre**, Hoole Bridge, run by the Chester Marketing Bureau Enterprise Agency, offers free advice to all business projects and there are office and workshop units available on a monthly licence basis. Tel: Chester 311474.

Chester – Residential City

CHESTER and its pleasing countryside offers ideal living conditions and leisure pursuits for all. A list of Estate Agents is available from the Chester Marketing Bureau.

Block salt maker at Lion
Salt Works, Marston

Cheshire Candle Workshops

A cottage in a Wirral village

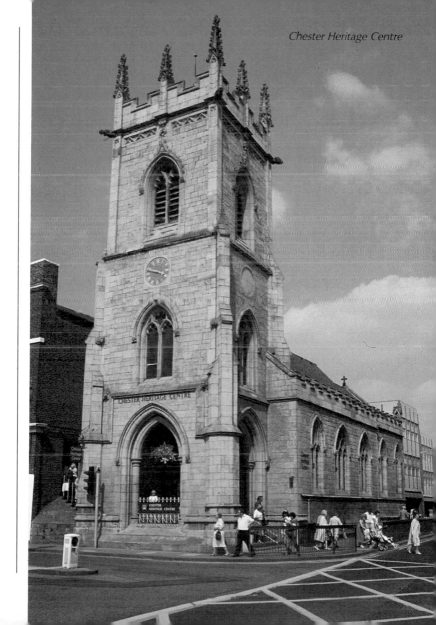

Chester Heritage Centre

CHESTER –
THE LEISURE SCENE

Chester Cathedral (see page 54).

Heritage Centres

Chester Heritage Centre (St Michael's Church): Bridge Street Row. Tel: 317948.
Open all the year, October–March – daily, except Wednesday, 1.30–
4.30 p.m. April–September – weekdays, except Wednesday, 10 a.m.–
5 p.m. Sundays 2–5 p.m. Admission charge. Discount for group bookings
of 10 and over.

Chester Visitor Centre: Vicars Lane. Tel: (0244) 313126 and 318916.
Tourist Information Centre and bureau de change. Video show on the
history of Chester (European languages available by arrangement). Life-
size reconstruction of the unique Rows in Victorian days, map and print
room showing growth of Chester since Roman times, craft shop, licensed
restaurant. Special family rates. Open 9 a.m.–9 p.m. seven days a week.
Parties welcomed.

St Mary's Centre
Formerly the Church of St Mary-on-the-Hill – founded *circa* A.D. 1100.
Present building fifteenth century. Fine Tudor roof, two seventeenth-
century monumental effigies, medieval glass, traces of wall painting. Now
used for exhibitions and meetings, base for educational visits to Chester.
Open to the public 2–4.30 p.m. weekdays or by arrangement.

Museums

Grosvenor Museum: Grosvenor Street (see page 39). Tel: 21616.
Admission free. Open weekdays 10 a.m.–5 p.m. Sundays 2–5 p.m.

King Charles' Tower
For opening hours, see *What's On in Chester*. Admission charge.

Water Tower
Closed.

Cheshire Military Museum: The Castle.
Open 9 a.m.–5 p.m. daily. Small admission charge.

Mouldsworth Motor Museum: Smithy Lane, Mouldsworth. (Six miles Chester.) Tel: Frodsham 31781.

Open every Sunday noon–6 p.m. Vintage, Post Vintage and Classic cars, cycles, etc. Admission charge. Parties by arrangement.

Toy Museum and Doll's Hospital: 42 Bridge Street.

Record Offices

Cheshire Record Office: The Castle, Chester. Tel: Chester 602574.

Hours of opening: Monday–Friday 9.45 a.m.–4.30 p.m. Evening openings by arrangement.

Chester City Record Office: Town Hall, Chester. Tel: Chester 40144, ext. 2108.

Hours of opening: Monday–Friday 9 a.m.–1 p.m., 2–5 p.m. Monday evening 5 7 p.m. (preferably by appointment).

Other Places of Interest

St John's Church and Ruins: Vicars Lane (see page 33).

Bishop Lloyd's House (see page 47). View by prior arrangement.

Cheshire Workshops: Candle Factory and Craft Centre, Burwardsley, Nr Tattenhall. Tel: Tattenhall 70401.

Visitors can watch craftsmen making candles and purchase these and many crafts at manufacturer's prices. Coach parties are advised to book in advance. Full catering facilities.

Zoological Gardens

Open every day from 10 a.m. (see page 70). Situated two miles north-east of City centre near A41 road, well signposted from major roads. Buses from near Town Hall and Railway Station. One of the world's best zoos with over 3000 animals in 110 acres of delightful landscaped gardens. Catering facilities to suit all tastes. Free car and coach park. Tel: 380280 for admission charges and further information.

Canal Trips

Horse-drawn narrowboat from Tower Wharf or Cow Lane Bridge. Parties by arrangement, bar and meals available. Tel: Chester 373950. (*The Chester Packet.*) One hour, three hour or longer trips with Snowy.

River Boating

Bithells Boats: The Groves, Chester (just off City Walls Road). Office: Eccleston Ferry, Huntingdon, Chester. Tel: 25394/316388.

Cruises on the River Dee to Eccleston Ferry and Ironbridge, sailing through Eaton Estate, home of the Duke of Westminster. Teas, bar, day and evening charter by arrangement. Rowing boats for hire by hour or day.

Williams Boat Company: The Groves, Chester. Tel: 314884.

Shropshire Union Canal

The Bridge of Sighs

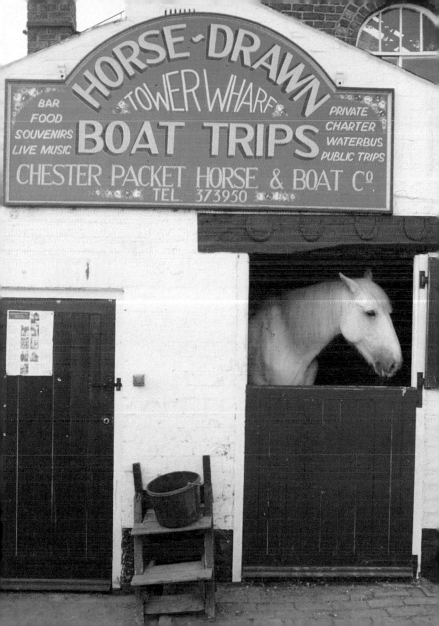

Entertainment

The Gateway Theatre: Hamilton Place, Chester. Box Office – Tel: 40393.
Professional repertory theatre presenting a wide variety of shows throughout the year. Generous discounts for senior citizens, children, students, parties. Book by American Express, Access and Barclaycard.

The Little Theatre Club: Gloucester Street, Newton. Tel: 22674 (evenings).

Odeon Cinema: Northgate Street. Tel: 24930. Cinemas 1, 2 and 3.

ABC: Foregate Street. Tel: 22931. Cinemas 1 and 2. Bingo.

Top Rank Club: Brook Street. Tel: 27165. Bingo.

Dancing
Modern Ballroom, Sequence, Latin American, Old Tyme, Disco, throughout the week, either classes, dinner-dances or social dancing. As these venues are subject to change, please see *What's On in Chester*.

Folk Clubs and Folk Dancing
Throughout the week, many clubs meet at various venues in and around Chester. As details change during the year, please see the monthly *What's On in Chester*.

Bridge: Deva Bridge Club, Watergate House, 85 Watergate Street, entrance Nicholas Street Mews. Tel: Club: 27818; Secretary: 319789.
Duplicate bridge, Tuesday, Wednesday and Saturday at 6.45 p.m. and Thursday at 7.15 p.m. Rubber bridge Monday and Friday afternoons.

Whist: Whist Drives – The Guildhall, Watergate Street. Tel: 20431 and St Barnabas Church Hall, Sibell Street. Tel: 47950.

Participation Sports

Fishing
Salmon, Migratory Trout, Trout and Coarse Fishing in the Rivers Dee and Clwyd and their tributaries. Licences obtainable from Welsh Water Authority, Cambrian Way, Brecon, Powys. Tel: Brecon 3181. Also from distributors throughout the area. Daily, weekly and seasonal licences available at appropriate fees.

Golf Courses
Westminster Park. Tel: 673071 (9 holes, par 3) at all times.
Chester Golf Club, Curzon Park. Tel: Club House: 675130; Secretary: 677760; Professional: 671185. 18 holes. No weekend or Bank Holiday visitors unless with member.
Eaton Golf Club, Eccleston. Tel: 674385. 18 holes.
Upton-by-Chester Golf Club. Tel: 381183. 18 holes. Special terms if under 21 and senior golfers.

Chester Zoo

Chester Zoo

Chester Zoo is situated just north of the City of Chester, and is readily accessible via the M53 and M56 motorways. The zoo occupies an area of land larger than the Liverpool Garden Festival site and in addition to being home to over 3000 animals, has some of the most spectacular gardens anywhere in this country.

The very reasonable admission charges are £2·50 per adult, £1·25 per O.A.P. and children 3–15 years (free under 3 years), and there are special rates for parties of 20 or more. This is now an all-inclusive price covering the cost of admission to the Tropical House (a zoological garden in itself) and the Aquarium. The car park is free too.

Chester Zoo is owned and controlled by the North of England Zoological Society, a charitable, scientific society where all the profits are ploughed back for the benefit of the livestock.

The zoo first opened to the public during 1931, and was made over to the North of England Zoological Society on 13 June 1934. At that time the zoo covered just ten acres, but has now expanded to cover over 130 acres of enclosures and gardens and in addition, the Society owns extensive areas of surrounding farmland.

At Chester Zoo the majority of the animals are exhibited in spacious natural enclosures amid delightful gardens. The gardens themselves are an added attraction with twenty-five full-time gardeners tending the landscaped grounds. The spring and summer bedding displays, involving the bedding out and changing of 160,000 plants annually, are most spectacular.

Chester Zoo has a world-wide reputation and many of the visitors come from overseas. The zoo has pioneered many modern methods of animal husbandry including keeping Gorillas, Orang-utans, and Chimpanzees on grassy islands only separated from the public by water-filled moats. The enormous Pachyderm House houses Elephants, Hippos, and Tapirs; pachyderm meaning 'thick skinned animal'. This building is also full of innovations, the Elephants have a huge outside island and are separated from the public by a flower border and dry ditch. Inside their spacious, centrally heated house, they are also separated from the public by a dry ditch and within the indoor enclosure there is a six-foot-deep bath.

The Tropical House is a completely unique building with a wealth of tropical vegetation including forty-foot-high banana trees. Visitors can walk among the thick vegetation and view the many species of free-flying Birds, see seventy species of Snakes and Lizards, look at Gorillas, and imagine that they are in one of the world's rapidly declining equatorial forests.

During recent years the zoo has also been at the forefront of zoo thinking and design. 1981 saw the opening of the Penguin Pool incorporating large viewing windows, so the Penguins can be seen swimming underwater. These lucky Penguins have a pool where the water is entirely cleaned and filtered every eight hours, and they are provided with a sandy beach and breeding caves.

Chester Zoo is also mindful of providing up-to-date facilities for the 800,000 people who visit annually. The new catering building 'The Jubilee Cafeteria' serves a wide range of food, and incorporates take-away facilities, hamburgers, and fast food.

The latest addition to the visitor facilities, is a young children's play area, designed on animal themes, with cut-out and model animals to amuse the youngsters and give their parents a rest. The Oakfield Restaurant has been completely re-furbished and the Acorn bar added and 'new look' shops are a feature of the Fountain area.

Chester Zoo has built up a world-wide reputation for breeding many rare species of animals, and has also pioneered many new and innovative designs for animal houses and enclosures. Future developments will take place with the objective of even further improving facilities for both the animals and the visitors. A house containing a nocturnal section with special facilities for the extremely rare Rodrigues Island Bats has recently opened to the public. The latest new animal exhibit is the Lion house and re-designed Lion enclosure; this development has opened to view the historical stable yard area which will be developed in the future.

Chester Zoo Tropical House

71

Slate Mines, Clwyd

Grange Cavern Military Museum, Clwyd

Medieval Fair, Ruthin

Velvet

Velvet

Cottage Craft

...Painted on Fabric

The Gateway Theatre

Hamilton Place, Chester.
Box Office — Tel: 40393, open 10.30 a.m.–8 p.m. (until 6 p.m. on days of no performance).
Performance times 7.30 p.m. Tuesday–Thursday, 8 p.m. Friday and Saturday.
Capacity 440.

Opened in 1968 the Gateway Theatre brings modern drama to a city long associated with the beginnings of English theatre, as Chester is the home of one of the few surviving cycles of medieval Mystery Plays.

Although situated in the heart of the old City of Chester, the Gateway Theatre serves a vast area, from the modern conurbations of Liverpool and Manchester, from the island of Anglesey to industrial Stoke on Trent, and from rural Oswestry to Buxton. The community which it serves is just as varied, including, during the summer months, a huge influx of visitors from all over the world.

To cater for this wide range of audience, the Gateway Theatre's policy is to offer the very best in every form of dramatic entertainment, from classics such as Shakespeare and Shaw, to modern comedies by the best contemporary writers, hard-hitting dramas about important social issues, specially devised community shows which tour around the area, and full-scale musical productions. Hits over the past few years include presentations as diverse as the children's fantasy *Wind in the Willows*, Claire Luckham's controversial *Trafford Tanzi*, Tom McClenaghan's powerful drama *Submariners*, and the specially commissioned *Landmarks* about agricultural Cheshire in the 30s.

In addition to the season of repertory productions in the main house, members of the permanent acting company also present a regular programme of lunchtime and late night shows, open rehearsals and after show discussions, seminars for students and a youth group. The Gateway is also the focal point for many other activities staged by the community; the prestigious Chester Summer Music Festival, Chester Symphony Orchestra concerts, Cheshire Dance Workshop annual young people's projects, events for Danceabout North-West, and a variety of amateur societies including its own Amateur Studio. The theatre also acts as a rendezvous for local artists and craftsmen, with poetry readings, puppet shows, exhibitions, and craft markets all part of the regular scene.

Once inside the Gateway Theatre you will find comfortable modern surroundings with a medium-sized auditorium (seating 440) where every seat offers an excellent and unimpeded view of the stage. The Gateway is alive throughout the day when the Coffee Shop is open for coffee and snacks and the licensed bar is open to the general public at lunchtime and each evening.

A visit to the Gateway Theatre during your stay in Chester will not only provide rewarding entertainment in itself, but also allows you to participate in the meeting of old and new traditions of drama in the City of Chester.

Northgate Arena
Leisure Centre

The Northgate Arena, which was opened in 1977, is undoubtedly one of the finest Leisure Centres in the country. There is always lots going on there, and its excellent facilities for spectators make it well worth a visit, even if you do not feel like taking part in any of the numerous activities which are available.

The heart of the building is a large free form Leisure Pool, which has a distinctly tropical atmosphere enhanced by palm-trees and other exotica, and which itself attracts over 300,000 visitors a year. The pool is overlooked by the cafeteria and one of the centre's two bars, and there is also a spectators' area by the side of the pool itself, where you can sit to watch the fun.

Another large spectators' gallery overlooks the Main Sports Hall, which is large enough to accommodate eight badminton courts and can be adapted very quickly for other sports, including tennis, 5-a-side football, hockey, netball, and volleyball. Three other halls cater for a wide variety of further activities including archery, judo, karate, table tennis, and various forms of dancing, and there is also a weight training room and four squash courts, which are again overlooked by a viewing gallery.

There is also a sauna and solarium, and conventional twenty five metre training pool to accommodate learners and serious swimmers.

Quite apart from all these sporting and recreational activities, the Arena is frequently used for other events, including exhibitions and trade fairs, social functions including 'Beach Parties' held beside the Leisure Pool, and a wide variety of entertainments ranging from fashion shows and concerts to circuses and professional wrestling.

Except for a short break at Christmas, the Arena is open seven days a week throughout the year, and visitors may be assured of a warm welcome. Opening times as follows:

| | Monday to Friday | | | | Saturday, Sunday and Bank Holidays | |
| | School Holidays | | Term Time | | | |
	From	Until	From	Until	From	Until
Leisure Pool	10 a.m.	9.30 p.m.	Noon	9.30 p.m.	10 a.m.	5.30 p.m.
Sauna	3 p.m.	10.30 p.m.	3 p.m.	10.30 p.m.	10 a.m.	5.30 p.m.
Dry Sports Facilities	10 a.m.	11 p.m.	10 a.m.	11 p.m.	10 a.m.	6 p.m.
Cafeteria	10 a.m.	10 p.m.	10 a.m.	10 p.m.	10 a.m.	5 p.m.

Bars — Normal licensing hours except closed on Saturday and Sunday evenings.

Jodrell Bank

Above and below: Tatton Park, Cheshire

Four pleasant excursions

Drive 1. Leaving Chester on the A41, Whitchurch Road, the village of **CHRISTLETON** lies two miles from the centre of the City. Christleton, or in Domesday, Cristetone, is suggestive of an early Christian settlement. Water from Abbot's Well at Christleton Bank was carried by pipe to a well within the cloisters of the Abbey at Chester; the Abbot's Well is now a pond. The Battle of Rowton Moor, 1645, was fought on a site in the parish of Christleton. Almshouses, designed by Mr John Scott, father of Sir Gilbert Scott, were built in 1865. The Roman bridges, three packhorse bridges along Plough Lane, formed part of the medieval highway.

ST PETER, WAVERTON, restored in 1845 and 1885; seventeenth-century font. A gravestone bears the inscription 'Esther wife of John Williams of Huxley died 1800, aged 95 – John died 1811, aged 105'.

On the A41 road about seven miles from Chester is the village of **HANDLEY** (High Pasture) with an old inn, the Calveley Arms. Parishioners of the Church of All Saints during the Siege of Chester in the Civil War are said to have been besieged in the tower by Cromwell's cavalry, the church being deliberately burnt in an effort to dislodge the parishioners. The south wall of the tower has a carving of a dog chasing a hare; the dog has its tail up and nose to the ground.

TATTENHALL, a pleasant old village. When the Church of St Alban was being rebuilt in 1869 (the sixteenth-century tower remains) 'the bones of a man of great stature' were found outside the north wall. Under his head was a coin or token; it was suggested this was to cover the toll over the 'Death River' and might point to a pre-Christian internment. There are Candle-making demonstrations at nearby Burwardsley.

BEESTON CASTLE, listed at the time of the Domesday Survey as being in the possession of Robert Fitz Hugh, Baron of Malpas, was garrisoned by Parliamentarians at the outbreak of the Civil War, but surrendered to the Royalists after nine months. After the Battle of Rowton Moor, it fell to the Parliament forces. The well has many interesting stories associated with it and has been explored to a depth of 360 feet in a search for Richard II's treasure which, tradition says, was thrown down the well before the Governor surrendered to Bolingbroke. Walk to the Castle summit to enjoy its famed and glorious views of the Cheshire Plains and Welsh Hills. Close by are **BICKERTON HILLS** and the **COPPERMINES** also the **SANDSTONE TRAIL** – a delightful picnic and walking area. $10\frac{1}{2}$ miles south-east of Chester.

MALPAS, one of Cheshire's oldest towns is the centre of a rich dairying district; the famous Cheshire cheeses are produced from milk of local herds. St Oswald's Church, is one of Cheshire's finest churches, built in the fourteenth and fifteenth centuries, with a fourteenth-century tower. The external wall of the aisles with the clerestory above form superb examples of the medieval craftsmen's art with the rich traceried windows, carved castellations and pinnacles. Both nave and chancel have fine panelled roofs and there are fifteenth-century stalls with misericords. In the south aisle is a chest over seven feet long, covered with flowery ironwork dating from the thirteenth century. Other treasures in the church are no less than four sedilias, one of which (fashioned with three grinning faces) is 600 years old. The east window is in memory of Bishop Heber, born in Malpas, who published many hymns (including From Greenland's Icy Mountains and Holy, Holy, Holy).

The nearby church of St Chad at **TUSHINGHAM** is a rare seventeenth-century treasure with its box pews and gallery. Open certain days each year.

Two miles from Malpas is **OVERTON HALL**. At the time of the Civil War, Sir William Brereton of Malpas, ardent supporter of the Parliamentary cause, drove back a party of Cheshire loyalist squires and troops at Oldcastle Heath. First of the family of Allport to settle here was Richard Allport, descended from a branch of the Allports of Cannock, Staffs. He appears to have acquired Overton towards the end of the reign of Elizabeth I. Richard Allport left £500 to found a school for boys and girls in Malpas. Malpas Almshouses were founded and endowed in 1676 by Sir William Brereton and built by Lord Cholmondeley in 1771. Overton Hall was a half-timbered gabled house, the moat enclosed about an acre of ground with a considerable range of farm buildings. It was restored in recent years by the present owners. There is a very attractive water garden and house, some rooms being heavily beamed. Cheshire cheese is made here. Visits by appointment only.

Three and a half miles north-west from Malpas are **SHOCKLACH**, where St Edith's Church is as the Normans built it, with rich carving, quaint bellcot and an amazing arch that is, in effect, but a shapeless hole in a wall; (Shocklach's isolation is recorded in testimony scratched on the east window with a diamond ring), and **TILSTON**, Church of St Mary, eighteenth-century gates with stone pillars carved with emblematic skull and crossbones, posts inscribed 1687 IP, IL. Church rebuilt 1877–78 except for tower and Stretton Chapel. Fine medieval roof, also altar rails in chancel consisting of slat balusters, dated 1677. Early Georgian pulpit. Cholmondeley Castle grounds and chapel are open Sundays, April–September.

Drive 2. **ECCLESTON** can be visited either by road (three miles) or river. First part of the name is of Celtic origin meaning 'tern' the farm or village – with a church. Eccleston is placed at the head of the list of the Baron of Kinnerton's estates in the Hundred of Broxton, in the Domesday Book. Watling Street passes through Eccleston to Aldford. This neat village is dominated by the splendid grounds of Eaton Hall, residence of the Duke of Westminster. The gardens of Eaton Hall, also the chapel and coach house with its fine collection of coaches, are open to the public on Easter Sunday, the Sunday of the Spring Bank Holiday, and one Sunday in July.

Leaving Chester via A483, the Wrexham Road, approximately four miles from Chester is **PULFORD**. St Mary's Church, 1881–84 built in the distinctive style of John Douglas, with shingled spire and tiny dormers. Nearby is **GRESFORD** where some fine glass is to be seen in the church.

The picturesque Holt/Farndon Bridge (fourteenth century) brings us to **FARNDON**. The name is Anglo-Saxon meaning Bracken Hill. King Edward the

The Holt/Farndon Bridge on the River Dee

Gasworth Hall

Elder died here A.D. 924. Cromwell's forces used St Chad's Church. Items of interest are the Armorial Window which is unique and shows the arms of the Gamull, Mainwaring and Barnston families; and the Steeplejack's prayer on the wall in the belfry. The village has some attractive magpie cottages. The Barnston Monument nearby commemorates Major Roger Barnston, noted for valour in the Crimean War. Farndon is famed for its Strawberry Crop. John Speed, cartographer, and the first English historian was born here in 1552. A Rush-bearing Service is held the second Sunday in July each year.

Four miles south-east of Chester is **BRUERA**. St Mary's Church was restored in 1896 with new additions. Bruera thought to have come from low latin for 'heath' but is essentially Norman and twelfth century in character. The church existed in Saxon times; some tenth-century masonry near doorway. Arms of Charles II are on the south wall. Ancient yew trees and remains of stone cross converted into sundial shaft dated 1693, head 1736. Lych gate is memorial to Countess Grosvenor, erected by parishioners and friends.

Drive 3. Leaving the City on the A51 road, **BARROW** has apparently changed very little, its field names and shapes show Anglo-Saxon influence. The attractively situated Church of St Bartholomew has had its own rectors since 1313 and was a parish church in 1291. In the fifteenth century, there seems to have been a complete rebuilding in the style of late Perpendicular Gothic. In 1671, the chancel was rebuilt. Of the roof, only the centre principal, of the hammer-beam type remains. Priest's doorway into the chancel was built up in the 1883 alterations. East window in the chancel, is by Kempe and his signature sign of peacock's feathers in the Angel's wings may be found in the wings of the Angel Gabriel in the scene of the Annunciation at the bottom of the window. Other items of interest are a good early Georgian chest of domestic construction; bell in the tower, cast in 1767, probably by Rudhall of Gloucester, weathervane erected in 1877 and sundial in the churchyard: tradition says that the base and shaft were once part of the old cross.

KELSALL. Bronze Age Celts are thought to have been the first inhabitants and there are traces of a Bronze Age Settlement at Kelsborrow Hill. In the vicinity is Peel Hall.

TARVIN. Attractive village with a very fine church. Tower of St Andrew dates from late fifteenth century, Tudor doorway on western side. First built in late twelfth century and belonged, with the Manor of Tarvin, to the Bishops of Lichfield and Coventry. Between arches in the south arcade, and placed over the capitals, are interesting carved heads, the faces peer down into the nave. The five-light east window in the north aisle is original. Fine 'Squint'. At the east end of the south aisle is the Bruen Chapel. John Bruen of Bruen Stapleford, owner of chapel of same name, was a well-known Calvinistic Puritan and lived at nearby Stapleford Hall. It is thought that his son John was partly responsible for the nave roof and his name is carved on one of the oak beams; interesting wooden memorial tablets. Near the church is a small school where the celebrated John Thomasen taught for thirty-six years; he died in 1740. Famed for his beautiful writing, he transcribed for Queen Anne the Icon Basilike of her royal grandfather. Legend associates nearby Hockenhall Hall, a Queen Anne House, with the 'Headless Woman' Inn at Duddon.

Drive 4. Taking the A56 (Hoole Road), one can visit **PLEMSTALL**, north-east of Mickle Trafford.

ST PETER, PLEMSTALL. Points of interest include a series of old Bibles: (i) 'Breeches' Bible 1608, (ii) King James' Bible 1611, (iii) Folio edition of Great Bible printed by 'Edwarde Whitchurche at the signe of the Sunne, Flete Street, London, 1549'. Fragments of ancient painted glass in several windows. Hammer-beam medieval roofing. Canopied churchwarden's pew 1697, three-decker pulpit, box pews. A fifteenth-century screen separates the chancel from the nave and the Barnston Chapel which is in the north side. The figures, the rood, and the enrichments on the top of these are the work of the Rev. J. H. Toogood, Rector from 1907 to 1944. He also made the altar, the reredos, the box pews, the choir stalls, the sanctuary panelling, the lectern, the war memorial, the baptistry screen, and the font cover. Church entirely rebuilt in the fifteenth century of sandstone. St Plegmund said to have lived here in a cell on 'The Isle of Chester' as a hermit (before being chosen by Alfred as his first instrument for reformation and consolidation of the State). Became Archbishop of Canterbury. A Holy Well, about 100 yards from the church, is said to have been a Druidical well before being put to Christian uses by Plegmund.

UPTON. Two miles from the City centre, previously farming country. Oakfield House, built 1883, since 1930 has been the world-famous zoo with its beautiful gardens. The Church of the Holy Ascension *circa* 1854, has two modern abstract stained-glass windows and a plague stone in its churchyard.

CHORLTON HALL. Continue from Upton along the main Chester to Liverpool road, turn right approximately two miles for Chorlton Hall. The earliest part of the house may be contemporary with a bell dated 1763. The house was restored after the Second World War. The original hall was probably demolished after a fire between 1831 and 1847. The coat of arms are those of James Wicksted Swan. Jacobean-style ceiling in dining room. In 1811 George Omerod, author of the celebrated *History of Cheshire*, was the owner and wrote the history here. View by appointment only.

BACKFORD. St Oswald's Church. Sixteenth-century Perpendicular-style tower has weird and ferocious gargoyles. Below these, the masons added their own carvings — a hen followed by her chickens; a dog chasing a rabbit; a goose apparently in flight; a fox on the prowl. The emblems recall the grant of an estate in the Backford parish by the abbot of St Werburgh's to his chief cook. Backford has one of the country's very few surviving aumbries (wall cupboards placed near the altar for a multitude of purposes). Many curious mason's marks are to be found in the church. Also a chained bible in the nave, 1617. Little Robert Barre was married to Elizabeth Rogerson in 1538, when barely three years old. Approximately nine miles further along the Liverpool Road at Port Sunlight is the famous **Lady Lever Art Gallery** collection.

CHESTER AS A TOURING CENTRE

Distances from Chester (miles)

Birmingham — 78	Leeds — 84
Blackpool — 72	Liverpool — 18
Bristol — 144	Llandudno — 47
Caernarvon — 73	London — 189
Edinburgh — 230	Manchester — 39
Lancaster — 70	Shrewsbury — 40

The City, once a military fortress of great strategic importance, has long been recognised as an equally important touring centre. Standing in a flat stretch of country midway between the Welsh Mountains and the Cheshire Hills, Chester has within easy reach an astonishing variety of scenery, varying between the essentially modern coastal resorts of Lancashire, Wirral, and North Wales to the wild moors of Derbyshire; from the pleasant agricultural and wooded landscape of the Cheshire hunting ground, to the rugged peaks and valleys of Snowdonia.

(Figures in brackets denote distances in miles from Chester)

West of Chester. This comprises North Wales. The recommended route to the coastal districts follows the road across the Grosvenor Bridge and via the Wrexham Road to the A55. St Winifred's Well at **Holywell** (17), via Northop, is a place of pilgrimage. Nearby are the fine ruins of Basingwerk Abbey. At **St Asaph** (28), there is an interesting cathedral and a fine parish church. After bearing right for half a mile the road turns left to **Abergele** (35). (Straight on, past Rhuddlan Castle, leads to Rhyl.) Beyond Abergele the road rises towards **Old Colwyn**, whence there is a magnificent view of **Colwyn Bay** (42); the beautiful Bodnant Gardens are close by; branching right just through Colwyn Bay, the road runs over the Little Orme, giving a delightful view of **Llandudno** (47). The toll-gates past the pier lead to a fine drive round the Great Orme, with a panoramic view of Penmaenmawr Mountain, the Menai Straits, Puffin Island, and beyond, Anglesey.

From the quaint old town of **Conway**, the Holyhead Road leads via **Bangor** and the Menai Bridge across the island of **Anglesey** (visit the nineteenth-century Penrhyn Castle); alternatively one may proceed south, preferably along the western side of the Conway River, to Betws-y-Coed, a place of outstanding beauty; thence the route to **Snowdonia** is via Capel Curig, whence one may proceed to **Caernarvon**, with its famous castle, either through the majestic pass of Llanberis and alongside the beautiful Llyn Padarn, or to the left through **Beddgelert**. Llanberis is the starting-point of the Snowdon Mountain Railway.

Further south are **Rhydymwyn** (14) via Mold; the Leet, a wonderful terraced walk above the River Alyn, leads to the Loggerheads Inn, whence Moel Fammau (1820 feet) can be ascended; **Denbigh** (26), with its historic castle in the heart of the Vale of Clwyd; and **Llangollen** (22), a famous beauty spot on the upper reaches of the Dee, where there are pleasure barges and boats along a picturesque stretch of canal to Berwyn, Horseshoe Falls, Valle Crucis Abbey, etc. Mention must be made of nearby Erddig, Plas Newydd, and Chirk Castle. A road over the spectacular Horseshoe Pass (1353 feet) leads across Llandegla Moors to Ruthin. **Bala** (45) and **Vyrnwy** (55) are peaceful lakes with lovely surroundings.

South of Chester. This covers the Dee Valley. **Eccleston Ferry** is 2 miles upstream from Chester. Further upstream are **Farndon** and **Holt** (9), reached via Foregate Street, Boughton, and Sandy Lane. The two villages are joined by a fine old bridge over the river. **Bangor-on-Dee** (17), **Overton** (19), and **Erbistock** (20) are all prettily situated on the Dee. The two former have picturesque bridges, while Erbistock Ferry is a famous beauty spot where good fishing is available, tickets being obtained at the Inn. Ellesmere (5½ miles south-east of Overton) is the centre of a miniature Lake District.

East of Chester **Delamere Forest** (10), via the Manchester Road, contains deep meres in the heart of thick pine-woods. The prettiest parts are east of Mouldsworth Station. There are excellent golf courses at Delamere and Sandiway.

TATTON PARK, Knutsford (off A50, A556). Magnificent house, former home of the Egertons for 300 years. Present house designed by Samuel and Lewis Wyatt, completed 1813. Furnished with Egertons' possessions, glass, china, paintings, stage coach, fire engine, vintage cars. Deer Park, self-guiding trails, horse riding, Japanese and Italian Gardens.

Other historic houses in the vicinity include Arley Hall, Dunham Massey, and Peover Hall, also the Salt Museum at Northwich.

North of Chester. The Wirral (via Parkgate Road or Liverpool Road), is a peninsula between the estuaries of the Dee and Mersey; **The Wirral Country Park**, **Burton**, **Parkgate**, and **Raby Mere**, each have a charm of their own. Near to Burton are the famous and lovely Ness Gardens, open all year. At **Hoylake** is the Royal Liverpool Golf Course. **Liverpool** (18), via Birkenhead, is interesting for its two tunnels under the Mersey, shipping and cathedrals.

On the road to Birkenhead, at **Port Sunlight** the **Lady Lever Art Gallery** (12½), (nearest Railway Station, Bebington). The Gallery was recently listed as one of the 200 most interesting Art Museums of the world. It contains the best assembly of English period furniture outside London; a worthwhile collection of paintings of the British School, including notable works by pre-Raphaelites; a collection of Wedgwood with an international reputation; five rooms of

Chinese pottery and porcelain; sculpture in many forms; English and oriental enamels; tapestries and needlework. Open on weekdays 10 a.m.–5 p.m., Sundays 2–5 p.m. Admission free.

Cheshire is ideal for those who love exploring old churches and anyone interested in this pastime is recommended to consult Raymond Richards' *Old Cheshire Churches* published by Batsford.

Thanks to the excellent transport facilities, a car is not essential to explore this beautiful country. During the season Crosville Motor Services Ltd, operate daily services, in addition to special day and half-day tours from Chester. Full particulars from Enquiry Bureau at the Bus Station. Lofty's Tours, Town Hall Square, provide a wide variety of day and half-day tours covering all central and North Wales and English beauty spots between Stratford-on-Avon, Buxton, and Windermere. Advance programmes, etc., available on request. Railway facilities are also available to the principal beauty spots.

Other City Itineraries covering 1 hour, half a day or a whole day are available on request from the Chester Marketing Bureau Ltd. Tel: (0244) 313126.

Civic Dignitaries

The Right Worshipful, The Mayor of Chester,
    Town Hall, Chester.
His Worship The Sheriff,
    Town Hall, Chester.

CITY OFFICERS
Tel: 40144
Chief Executive & Director of Finance
City Secretary & Solicitor
The Treasurer
Director of Technical Services
Chief Engineer
Chief Planning Officer
Chief Housing Officer
Director of Environmental Health
Transport Manager
City Archivist
Mayor's Secretary

Curator, Grosvenor Museum. Tel: 21616
Manager, Northgate Arena. Tel: 380444

ROYAL VISITS TO CHESTER

Since late Anglo-Saxon times, Chester has enjoyed strong links with the Monarchy. In the Middle Ages, most Royal visits to Chester were concerned with political or military events; particularly the English conquest of North Wales. In modern times, the Sovereign; the Prince of Wales, who is also Earl of Chester; and other members of the Royal Family, have usually visited the City on more pleasurable occasions. The following is a selection of the most notable Royal visits:

973	King Edgar came to Chester to meet the kings of several vassal states in the north and west of Britain. Tradition asserts that they rowed him on the River Dee.
1069–70	William I invaded Cheshire, and began the building of Chester Castle.
1241–83	Henry III, and his son Edward I, frequently visited Chester, the main base for their operations against North Wales.
1301	Edward of Caernarfon, first Royal Prince of Wales and Earl of Chester, came to the City to receive the homage of many of his tenants.
1353	Edward, the Black Prince, son of Edward III, came to Chester, having heard 'grievous clamours and complaints . . . which cannot be fittingly redressed without his presence'.
1399	Henry Bolingbroke, Duke of Lancaster, later Henry IV, invaded Cheshire. He later brought Richard II to Chester before taking him to London, where the king was deposed.
1499	Arthur, Prince of Wales and Earl of Chester, son of Henry VII, visited Chester, and presented a silver badge to the Smiths, Cutlers, and Plumbers Company.
1617	James I visited Chester, when Members of the City Corporation contributed £100 as a present for him.
1642, 1645	Charles I visited Chester twice during the Civil War. On the second occasion, he witnessed his army's defeat at Rowton Moor.
1687	James II was entertained by the Corporation, and touched 350 persons in the Cathedral, for the King's Evil.
1832	Princess Victoria, niece of William IV, opened and named the Grosvenor Bridge.

1869	Albert Edward, Prince of Wales and Earl of Chester, later Edward VII, opened the newly built Chester Town Hall.
1914	George V opened the Albert Wood Wings of the Infirmary; and granted the title 'Royal' to the Infirmary.
1926	Edward, Prince of Wales and Earl of Chester, later Edward VIII, reviewed a rally of Scouts and Guides on the Roodee, and laid a wreath at the Cathedral War Memorial.
1946	George VI and Queen Elizabeth visited Chester as part of a tour of Cheshire.
1957	H.M. Queen Elizabeth II opened County Hall, and presented colours to three battalions of the Cheshire Regiment.
1960	H.M. Queen Elizabeth, The Queen Mother, opened the new King's School on Wrexham Road.
1962	H.R.H. Princess Margaret attended a performance of the Chester Mystery Plays on the Cathedral green.
1967	H.R.H. The Duchess of Gloucester (Princess Alice) opened the new Cheshire Constabulary Headquarters.
1971	H.R.H. Prince Charles, Prince of Wales and Earl of Chester, paid his first official visit to Chester.
1973	H.R.H. The Prince of Wales and Earl of Chester, was admitted an Honorary Freeman of the City of Chester.
1975	H.R.H. The Duke of Gloucester opened the new Bell Tower of Chester Cathedral, and the Chester Heritage Centre; and inspected buildings restored for European Architectural Heritage Year.
1979	During Chester's 1900th Anniversary celebrations, H.R.H. The Prince of Wales and Earl of Chester, visited the exhibition 'Chester and the Monarchy' at the Town Hall, and attended a performance, in Chester Cathedral, of 'The Chester Tales' on 5 July; and H.M. The Queen and H.R.H. Prince Philip, Duke of Edinburgh, attended a service of Thanksgiving in the Cathedral, on 2 November.
1984	The Prince and Princess of Wales visited Chester Town Hall and the West Cheshire Hospital, which Her Royal Highness renamed Countess of Chester Hospital, on 30 May.

GENERAL INFORMATION

Population: 116,657.
Area: 44,810 hectares.
Rateable Value: £18,478,800.
Rates: 1984/85.
General Rate: Domestic, 174p in £. Commercial, 192.5p in £.
Elevation: 90 feet.
Subsoil: Sandstone, gravel, light clay.
Climate: Fairly mild, average rainfall over last ten years, 26.7 inches.
Early Closing: 6-day trading – some close on Wednesdays.
Public Market: The Forum.
Cattle Market: Bumpers Lane, Tuesday and Thursday periodically.
Horse Sales: 2nd and 4th Wednesday in month, at Beeston Smithfield.
Tel: Chester 317833.

Public Libraries

Town Hall Square, Northgate Street. Tel: 312935. Hours (all departments):
Monday, Tuesday, Thursday, Friday 9.30 a.m.–8 p.m., Wednesday 9.30 a.m.–
5 p.m., Saturday 9.30 a.m.–1 p.m.
The Reference Library is freely available to all and contains a fine collection of
material relating to the history of Chester and Cheshire. Books may be
borrowed from the Lending Library on production of current library tickets
issued by any public library authority in the country.
Also, libraries at Lache Park Avenue; Hoole Road; Wealstone Lane, Upton;
Green Lane, Vicar's Cross; Bishops High School, Vaughans Lane; Western
Avenue, Blacon; Heber High School, Malpas.

Car Parks

Princess Street Complex at rear of Town Hall (entrances off inner ring road and
Princess Street); Trinity Street (Short Stay Shoppers' car park); Little Roodee (off
Castle Drive); Shopping Precinct, Newgate Street; Pepper Street; Gorse Stacks;
Weaver Street/Nicholas Street; Cuppin Street; New Crane Street; St Anne
Street; Garden Lane/Lorne Street; Northgate Arena. Free parking at all the
above locations on Sunday mornings with the exception of Gorse Stacks, Little
Roodee, Princess Street Complex, Newgate Street and Pepper Street.
The County Officers' Car Park, The Castle (Saturdays only).
The following are free all week: Charles Street (off Brook Street); Steam Mill

Street (off Boughton); Christleton Road; Northgate Arena, Victoria Road (for Arena users).

Airports

Liverpool, 6 miles from Liverpool City Centre, 24 miles from Chester by road via Mersey Tunnels or Widnes, Runcorn and M56. Daily services from Liverpool to London, Belfast, Dublin, etc.

Manchester International Airport, 10 miles from Manchester City Centre, 35 miles from Chester by road M53, M56. **Crosville's Townlynx coach, Manchester, Manchester Airport (73 minutes), Chester, four times a day.**

Transport

Chester City Transport: for timetables, apply to Transport Manager, Chester City Transport, Station Road. Tel: 40144. Services operate from Bus Exchange Point, Princess Street (near Town Hall) to Railway Station via St Werburgh Street, Eastgate Street, Foregate Street and City Road. City and environs bus tour during summer months with commentary.

Crosville Motor Services Limited: for timetables, apply to Crosville Publicity Department, Crane Wharf or Delamere Street Bus Station Enquiry Office, Tel. 381515. Services operate from Bus Exchange, St John Street, St Werburgh Street.

Long Distance Bus Services, Delamere Street/George Street Bus Station – Crosville/National Services, including London, Manchester Airport, Shrewsbury, etc. See also under Manchester Airport.

Motor Coach Tours

Crosville Motor Services Limited, Lofty's Tours Limited, Huxley's, Threapwood.

Banks

Barclays Bank Limited, 35 Eastgate Street; 30 St Werburgh Street; 2 Derby Place, Hoole; 22 High Street, Saltney.

Lloyds Bank Limited, 8 Foregate Street; 84 Weston Grove, Upton-by-Chester; 138 Christleton Road; Chester Road, Kelsall; Station Road, Tattenhall; Main Street, Tarvin.

Midland Bank Limited, 47 Eastgate Street; 47 Hoole Road, Hoole; 97 Boughton; MANWEB Administrative Centre, Knutsford Way, Sealand Industrial Estate. Midland Bank Trust Company Limited, 25 Lower Bridge Street.

National Westminster Bank, 33 Eastgate Street; 30 Boughton; 10–12 Foregate Street; 2 Faulkner Street, Hoole; The Parade, Blacon; 15 Handbridge.

Williams and Glyn's Bank Limited, 15 Foregate Street.

Trustee Savings Bank, 29 Grosvenor Road; 13 Hoole Road; 8 Boughton; 145 Long Lane, Upton.

North West Securities Limited, North West House, City Road.

Places of Worship

Church of England
The Cathedral (**see** p 54); St John the Baptist, Vicar's Lane; St Peter's, The Cross; St Mary-without-the-Walls, Handbridge; Christ Church, Gloucester Street; St Mark's, Hough Green; St Paul's, Boughton; St Thomas of Canterbury, Parkgate Road; All Saints, Hoole Road; Holy Trinity-without-the-Walls, Blacon; Church of the Holy Ascension, Church Lane, Upton; St James, Christleton.

Roman Catholic
St Francis, Grosvenor Street; St Werburgh, Grosvenor Park Road; St Anthony, High Street, Saltney; St Theresa, Blacon; St Clare, Downsfield Road, Lache; St Columba, Plas Newton.

Methodist
Wesley, St John Street; Tarvin Road, Boughton; Garden Lane; Hamilton Street, Hoole; High Street, Saltney; Piper's Ash.

Baptist
Westminster Road, Hoole; Francis Street; Penri Memorial, Gorse Stacks (Welsh); Zion Tabernacle, Grosvenor Park Road.

United Reformed Church (Congregational)
Handbridge; Whipcord Lane; Hoole Road, Hoole; Albion Street (Welsh); Saughall Road, Blacon; Heath Road, Upton; Green Lane, Vicar's Cross.

United Reformed Church (Presbyterian)
St Andrew's, Newgate Street.

Church of Christ
Upper Northgate Street; Hough Green.

Kingsway Chapel
Grasmere Road, Newton.

The New Church
Brook Lane/Dickson's Drive, Newton.

Presbyterian Church of Wales
City Road (English); St John Street (Welsh).

Salvation Army
St Anne Street.

Unitarian
Matthew Henry Chapel, Blacon Point Road, Blacon.

First Church of Christ Scientist
St Olave Street, Lower Bridge Street.

Society of Friends (Quakers)
Union Walk, Frodsham Street.

Education
Education Offices, Wellington Road, Ellesmere Port. Tel: 051–355 7133.

Colleges

Chester College. A Church of England College of Higher Education, affiliated to Liverpool University for B.Ed. and B.A. degrees together with diploma courses (full-time and part-time) for teachers, social workers, and the general public. Founded 1839, 850 full-time and 250 part-time students. For further information, apply to the Admissions Secretary, Chester College, Cheyney Road, Chester.

Chester College of Further Education. For further information apply to the Principal, Chester College of Further Education, Eaton Road, Chester (Chester District).

College of Law, Christleton. For details apply to The Secretary.

Schools

Secondary Comprehensive Schools

Blacon High School (11–18 years).
Catholic High School (11–18 years).
Kingsway High School (11–18 years).
Queen's Park High School (11–18 years).
Christleton County High School (11–18 years).
Chester Bishops Bluecoat CE Aided High School (11–18 years).
Bishop Heber County High School, Malpas (11–18 years).
Upton-by-Chester County High School (11–18 years).

Primary

2 Nursery Schools.
15 Infant Schools (5–7 years).
37 Primary Schools (5–11 years).
12 Junior Schools (7–11 years).

Special

Dee Banks School, Moston School, Dorin Park School.

Independent Schools

Abbey Gate School, Victoria Road ($3\frac{1}{2}$–12 years).
Abbey Gate College, Saighton Grange, (11–17 years).
Firs School, Newton Lane (4–11 + years).
Hammond School, Hoole Bank (11–16 years).
Hollybank School, Abbots Hayes, Liverpool Road (2–15 years).
King's School, Wrexham Road (Boys, 8–18 years).
Merton House School, 27 Liverpool Road ($4\frac{1}{2}$–12 years).
Queen's School, City Walls Road (Girls, 11–18 years).
Queen's Preparatory and Junior Schools, Liverpool Road (4–11 years).

Youth Centres

Blacon Youth Centre, Melbourne Road.
Bluecoat Youth Centre, Upper Northgate Street.

Lache Youth Centre, Hawthorne Road.
The New Scene Youth Centre, Newton Lane.
Square One Youth Centre, Thackeray Drive, Vicar's Cross.
The Park Youth Centre, Park Primary School, Tattenhall.

Cheshire Outdoor Education Centres

Burwardsley Outdoor Education Centre, Tattenhall.
Beeston Outdoor Education Centre, Beeston, Tarporley, Cheshire.

Department of Employment

Unemployment Benefit Office, Norroy House, Nuns Road. Tel: 315571.

Manpower Services Commission

Employment Service Division, Jobcentre, 86 Northgate Street. Tel: 312881.

Post Offices

Head Post Office, Station Road. Last collection: Monday–Friday 9.45 p.m., Saturday 1 p.m. St John Street; 48 Brook Street; Northgate Street; Watergate Street.

Hospitals

Royal Infirmary, St Martin's Way. Tel: 315500.
City Hospital, Hoole Lane. Tel: 315500.
Countess of Chester Hospital, Liverpool Road. Tel: 315500.
Countess of Chester Hospital, Psychiatric Wing. Tel: 379333.
Ellesmere Port Hospital, Ellesmere Port. Tel: 051–355 2345.
Manor Hospital, Great Sutton. Tel: 051–339 3222.
Grosvenor Nuffield Hospital, Wrexham Road (private). Tel: 311655.
Red Cross, Vicar's Lane, Secretary. Tel: 23375.
St John's Ambulance, Divisional Superintendent. Tel: 673485, 672524.

Local Newspapers

Chester Observer and *Chester Chronicle*, on sale Friday.
Chester Express, circulated Wednesday, free.
Chester Mail, circulated Wednesday, free.
Offices of all above newspapers, Bridge Street.
Evening Leader, 33A Lower Bridge Street.

Police

Cheshire Constabulary, Castle Esplanade, Chester. Tel: 315432.

A SHORT READING LIST

Addleshaw, G.W.O. — *The Pictorial History of Chester Cathedral*, 1969, and later editions.

* Boulton, Helen E., ed. — *The Chester Mystery Plays*, 2nd edition, 1980.

Burne, R. V. H. — *Chester Cathedral*, 1958.

Burne, R. V. H. — *The Monks of Chester*, 1962.

* Chester City Record Office — *Chester and the Monarchy*, 1979.

* Chester City Record Office — *Chester Town Hall*, 1979.

* Chester Heritage Centre — *The Church and Parish of St Michael, Chester*, 1981.

* Groombridge, Margaret J. — *Guide to the Charters, Plate, and Insignia of the City of Chester*, [1950].

Harris, B. E. — *Chester*, 1979.

* Harris, B. E. — *The History of the County Palatine of Chester. A Short Bibliography and Guide to Sources*, 1983.

Hemingway, J. — *History of the City of Chester*, 1831.

Hughes, T. — *The Stranger's Handbook to Chester*, 1856 and later editions; reprinted 1972.

* Insall, D. W., and Associates — *Chester: A Study in Conservation*, 1968.

* Kennett, Annette M. — *Chester Schools*, 1973.

* Kennett, Annette M., ed. — *Chester: Nineteen Hundred Years of History*, 1979.

* Kennett, Annette M. — *Chester and the River Dee.* An Illustrated History of Chester and its Port, 1982.

Morris, R. H. — *Chester in the Plantagenet and Tudor Reigns*, [1894].

Ormerod, G. — *History of the County Palatine and City of Chester*, 2nd edition, by T. Helsby, 1881.

* Palliser, D. M., ed. — *Chester: Contemporary Descriptions by Residents and Visitors*, 2nd edition, 1980.

Strickland, T. J. and Davey, P. J., eds. — *New Evidence for Roman Chester*, 1978.

* Strickland, T. J.	*Roman Chester*, 1984.
Thompson, F. H.	*Deva: Roman Chester*, 1959.
University of London Institute of Historical Research	*Victoria History of Cheshire*, vol. 2, 1979, includes the Parliamentary history of Chester, and tables of population. Vol. 3, 1980, contains histories of religious houses, Chester Cathedral, and the King's and Queen's Schools.

Many articles on Chester's history have appeared in the *Journal of the Chester Archaeological Society*, published since 1850; and in *The Cheshire Sheaf*, published between 1878 and 1978. Both may be consulted in the Chester City Record Office, where there are indexes to the *Journal*, and to the Chester material in the *Sheaf*. Copies of all the works cited here are available for consultation in the City Record Office; those marked with an asterisk may be purchased at the Tourist Information Centre, Chester Visitor Centre, the Chester City Record Office, the Chester Heritage Centre, or the Grosvenor Museum.

Chester in Books: some additional and attractive reading matter on **Chester** and its countryside is available from local booksellers.

ANNUAL EVENTS

January	Dance Festival.
February, March, April, May	Chester Music Festival (Competitive): Dance, Speech and Drama, Pianoforte, Instrumental Solo, Choirs and Vocal Solo.
March	North of England Head of River Race.
May	Regatta.
May	Chester Folk Festival.
May	Beating Retreat.
June	Chester Tattoo.
May, July, August	Chester Races.
June	Cheshire Show.
June–July	Chester at Leisure Fortnight, including Raft Race.
July	Llangollen International Music Festival.
July–August	Chester Summer Music Festival (internationally famous).
August 1985	Tudor Chester.
December	Carols Round the Christmas Tree.

INDEX